PhpStorm Cookbook

Discover over 80 recipes to learn how to build and test
PHP applications efficiently using the PhpStorm IDE

Mukund Chaudhary

Ankur Kumar

PUBLISHING

BIRMINGHAM - MUMBAI

PhpStorm Cookbook

First published: December 2014

Production reference: 1221214

Published by Packt Publishing Ltd.
Livery Place
35 Livery Street
Birmingham B3 2PB, UK.
ISBN 978-1-78217-387-8

www.packtpub.com

Cover image by Gagandeep Sharma (er.gagansharma@gmail.com)

Credits

Authors

Mukund Chaudhary

Ankur Kumar

Reviewers

Shahin Katebi

Kirill Roskolii

Shuvankar Sarkar

Commissioning Editor

Ashwin Nair

Acquisition Editor

Kevin Colaco

Content Development Editor

Sharvari Tawde

Technical Editors

Manan Badani

Pankaj Kadam

Copy Editor

Sarang Chari

Project Coordinator

Judie Jose

Proofreaders

Maria Gould

Stephen Silk

Katherine Tarr

Indexer

Tejal Soni

Production Coordinator

Aparna Bhagat

Cover Work

Aparna Bhagat

About the Authors

If being knowledgeable and presentable is uniqueness, **Mukund Chaudhary** is the correct person to be termed unique. Having started his career primarily in programming, he developed an interest in management that led him to pursue an MBA even after obtaining an engineering degree.

Mukund is a team worker and is currently working as a technical product manager at Nityo Infotech Services Pvt. Ltd., New Delhi. His knowledge combined with the presentation skills give him an edge over his contemporaries. He likes to spend his spare time writing or with family. You can follow him on Twitter at `https://twitter.com/mukund002`.

I take this opportunity to extend my thanks to the strong and warm support provided to me by my family—my parents, my better half, and my grandfather. It was their motivation that led me to complete writing my first book ever.

My friends also deserve a fair share of the thanks. They were always there by my side to provide positive ideas and constructive criticism, as a result of which I was able to complete this tough task with much ease. I would also like to give a special thanks to the editors and all the people who played a part in the publishing of this book.

Ankur Kumar is an apt example of a dark horse. He often outperforms his contemporaries when he is in full flow. A team mentor by role, Ankur works for Nityo Infotech Services Pvt. Ltd. His seat remains vacant most of the time as he remains busy solving the problems of his teammates. Ankur has around 6 years of experience in the IT industry. He has worked in various roles for various companies across the globe. He has been working on LAMP stack for the last 3 years continually. He finds programming a challenge worth taking up and enjoys the one-to-one tussle with problem solving.

Ankur is a strong believer of the fact that a human should always make other humans happy in one way or the other. Even in the middle of tough tasks, he can be found cracking jokes (often on himself) to make the work environment lighter.

If someone is to be acknowledged, it should be the Almighty. It was due to his will that I got the opportunity to convert myself into a part-time author. Somewhere at the back of my mind, I always had this wish to impart the knowledge I gained all these years solving programming problems.

I sincerely thank everyone involved in the book-writing process to have understood the ideas that I wished to convey. The editors do deserve a fair share of thanks for their hard work.

My parents, my sister, and my better half are my real strength, and I will always be thankful to the Almighty for giving me a life worth living.

About the Reviewers

Shahin Katebi is a software architect and developer with 10 years of experience in creating apps for various platforms (Mac, iOS, Windows, and the Web). He works as a mobile solutions consultant with different companies in the business, marketing, and technical fields and also works with a few start-up teams worldwide. He teaches iOS/Mac OS development and as a mentor at Startup Weekend events, he helps start-up teams grow their own business. He is the founder and team leader at Seeb Co. (`http://seeb.co/`), a creative mobile app development organization that creates apps for customers around the world. He also runs and accelerates multiple start-up businesses in various fields worldwide.

Shahin has also helped with fact checking and technical editing for books such as *iOS and OS X Network Programming Cookbook, Jon Hoffman, Packt Publishing*.

> I want to say a very special thanks to my beloved Nafiseh for her precious presence and support.

Kirill Roskolii is a passionate open source PHP/Drupal backend developer. He started his programming career as a freelance web developer in 2006. Afterwards, he created a small web studio with a couple of schoolmates and worked in ShvetsGroup, Kiev. Currently, he works as a lead Drupal backend developer in Trellon, LLC, maintaining CRM Core and a few other projects on Drupal.org.

> I want to thank my wife for her support not only during the work on this book, but my entire life.

Shuvankar Sarkar is senior software engineer experienced in C#, .NET, PHP, and web development. He maintains his blog at `http://shuvankar.com`. Apart from official work, he is involved with several hobby projects (for example, `http://tencovid.com`). He is a member of Teamencoder (`http://teamencoder.com`). You can follow him on Twitter at `@sonu041`. Shuvankar is interested in computer security and Rubik's Cube.

I would like to thank my family for making my life easier and full of happiness.

www.PacktPub.com

Support files, eBooks, discount offers, and more

For support files and downloads related to your book, please visit www.PacktPub.com.

Did you know that Packt offers eBook versions of every book published, with PDF and ePub files available? You can upgrade to the eBook version at www.PacktPub.com and as a print book customer, you are entitled to a discount on the eBook copy. Get in touch with us at service@packtpub.com for more details.

At www.PacktPub.com, you can also read a collection of free technical articles, sign up for a range of free newsletters and receive exclusive discounts and offers on Packt books and eBooks.

https://www2.packtpub.com/books/subscription/packtlib

Do you need instant solutions to your IT questions? PacktLib is Packt's online digital book library. Here, you can search, access, and read Packt's entire library of books.

Why subscribe?

- ▶ Fully searchable across every book published by Packt
- ▶ Copy and paste, print, and bookmark content
- ▶ On demand and accessible via a web browser

Free access for Packt account holders

If you have an account with Packt at www.PacktPub.com, you can use this to access PacktLib today and view 9 entirely free books. Simply use your login credentials for immediate access.

Table of Contents

Preface   1
Chapter 1: Cooking with PhpStorm   7
  Introduction   7
  Showing/hiding views   8
  Customizing a view   10
  Accessing any project file   16
  Maximizing views and editors   17
  Going back to the previous editor   18
  Going back to the previous edit location   19
  Linking views to editors   20
  Creating a key binding   21
  Creating a bookmark   22
  Restoring deleted resources   23
  Customizing with PhpStorm   26
  Adding an include path   29
  Excluding unwanted directories from the index   30
  Using code completion   32
Chapter 2: PHP Development   35
  Introduction   35
  Creating a PHP project using Composer   36
  Creating an empty project   41
  Reusing an existing project   41
  Creating a new PHP class   42
  Creating a new PHP method   45
  Adding the getter/setter methods   48
  Creating delegate methods   50
  Surrounding code with control structures   52

Finding the matching brace	56
Commenting out a section of code and PHPDoc	58
Creating a working set	62
Creating TODO tasks	64

Chapter 3: Refactoring and Building — **67**

Introduction	67
Renaming elements	68
Copying elements	72
Moving elements	73
Moving a method	74
Moving a variable	75
Deleting elements	77
Searching code in a project	79
Comparing files	84
Restoring elements using comparison	87
Setting the run configuration	88
Running your code	92

Chapter 4: Integrating Framework — **95**

Introduction	95
Cooking with Symfony	96
Creating a controller with Symfony	101
Creating a model with Symfony	103
Creating a view with Symfony	106
Creating a model with the Yii framework	107
Creating a controller with the Yii framework	109
Creating a view with the Yii framework	110
Creating a model with the Zend framework	111
Creating a controller with the Zend framework	113
Creating a view with the Zend framework	114

Chapter 5: Testing and Debugging — **119**

Introduction	119
Installing PHPUnit	120
Test case in PHPUnit	122
Testing an application with PHPUnit	124
Starting a debugging session	127
Setting a breakpoint	129
Configuring breakpoint conditions	130
Creating exception breakpoints	132
Stepping through your code	134

Running to a line of code selected   136
Watching expressions and variables   138
Changing code on the fly   139
Code coverage in PhpStorm   140

Chapter 6: Using PhpStorm in a Team   **145**
Introduction   145
Getting a VCS server   146
Creating a VCS repository   148
Connecting PhpStorm to a VCS repository   150
Storing a PhpStorm project in a VCS repository   151
Committing files to the VCS repository   154
Updating code from a VCS repository   157
Synchronizing your code with the VCS repository   160
Examining the VCS repository   162
Checking projects out of a VCS repository   165
Creating code patches   168
Creating VCS tags or branches   172
Creating a task for the team   176

Chapter 7: PhpStorm and Phing   **179**
Introduction   179
Connecting Phing and PhpStorm   180
Catching Phing build file syntax problems   183
Building a PhpStorm application using Phing   186
Using a different build file   188
Doing wonders with Phing   190
Using the Phing build view   194

Chapter 8: Cooking Library Plugins   **197**
Introduction   197
Creating a library plugin   198
Refining the plugin   202
Configuring the plugin with PhpStorm   204
Code hinting for the plugin   205

Chapter 9: Code Quality Analysis   **209**
Introduction   209
Mess detector and PhpStorm   211
Code sniffer and PhpStorm   219
Locating code duplicates   223
Code formatting and arrangement   226

Index   **233**

Preface

PhpStorm is a smart PHP IDE that gets your code and understands its structures. It provides code autocompletion, refactoring, syntax highlighting, and much more. PhpStorm makes debugging and testing really easy, especially with debugger configuration validation.

PhpStorm Cookbook contains several tutorials that will allow you to run PHP development at a good pace by helping you test and debug, which is often ignored by developers.

The book starts off focusing on how to cook using PhpStorm, gives you an overview of PHP development, and then dives deep into the details of refactoring and building your project using the PhpStorm IDE. After that, it moves to integrating frameworks and testing and debugging them. We then move on to using PhpStorm in a team, using Phing and cooking plugins. We conclude that this book will be of a great help to a PHP programmer who loves to use IDE and looks forward to working faster.

What this book covers

Chapter 1, Cooking with PhpStorm, gives you a quick overview about accessing a project, customizing a view, moving to the previous and next editor locations, and more.

Chapter 2, PHP Development, covers PHP classes; methods, including the getter/setter method; code blocks; commenting; and more.

Chapter 3, Refactoring and Building, includes renaming, copying, moving, and deleting elements; it includes code searching, comparing, and setting the run configuration.

Chapter 4, Integrating Framework, covers the need for a framework and how frameworks such as Symphony and Yii work with PhpStorm.

Chapter 5, Testing and Debugging, gives you an overview about installing PHPUnit, testing an application, setting a breakpoint, changing code on the fly, and much more.

Chapter 6, Using PhpStorm in a Team, includes creating a CVS repository, connecting PhpStorm to a CVS repository, committing a file, checking out projects, and much more.

Chapter 7, PhpStorm and Phing, gives you an overview of connecting Phing to PhpStorm, building an application, setting the Phing editor option, and more.

Chapter 8, Cooking Library Plugins, is about validating a plugin, code hinting for the plugin, and more.

Chapter 9, Code Quality Analysis, covers the mess detector and the code sniffer; it also covers locating code duplicates and code formatting and rearrangement.

What you need for this book

This book assumes you have prior knowledge of PHP and you have a computer with Apache, PHP, and PhpStorm IDE installed.

Who this book is for

This book is for all levels of web application developers who look forward to working faster and efficiently using PhpStorm IDE. It assumes that readers have prior knowledge of PHP development using the LAMP/WAMP environment; however, this book focusses on LAMP.

Sections

This book contains the following sections:

Getting ready

This section tells us what to expect in the recipe and describes how to set up any software or any preliminary settings needed for the recipe.

How to do it...

This section characterizes the steps to be followed to "cook" the recipe.

How it works...

This section usually consists of a brief and detailed explanation of what happened in the previous section.

There's more...

It consists of additional information about the recipe in order to make the reader more anxious about the recipe.

See also

This section may contain references to the recipes.

Conventions

In this book, you will find a number of styles of text that distinguish between different kinds of information. Here are some examples of these styles, and an explanation of their meaning.

Code words in text, database table names, folder names, filenames, file extensions, pathnames, dummy URLs, user input, and Twitter handles are shown as follows: "If a folder is provided in include path, it will be helpful in auto completion for `include()`, `require()`, and so on."

A block of code is set as follows:

```
class Dish {
/**
* @param string $dishName The name of the dish
*/
protected function addSalt(){ }
}
```

A command-line input or output is shown as:

```
svnadmin create /path/to/your/repo/
```

New terms and **important words** are shown in bold. Words that you see on the screen, in menus or dialog boxes for example, appear in the text like this: "To turn this feature on, you need to select the checkbox adjacent to **Sort lookup items lexicographically**."

 Warnings or important notes appear in a box like this.

 Tips and tricks appear like this.

Reader feedback

Feedback from our readers is always welcome. Let us know what you think about this book—what you liked or may have disliked. Reader feedback is important for us to develop titles that you really get the most out of.

To send us general feedback, simply send an e-mail to `feedback@packtpub.com`, and mention the book title via the subject of your message.

If there is a topic that you have expertise in and you are interested in either writing or contributing to a book, see our author guide on `www.packtpub.com/authors`.

Customer support

Now that you are the proud owner of a Packt book, we have a number of things to help you to get the most from your purchase.

Downloading the example code

You can download the example code files for all Packt books you have purchased from your account at `http://www.packtpub.com`. If you purchased this book elsewhere, you can visit `http://www.packtpub.com/support` and register to have the files e-mailed directly to you.

Errata

Although we have taken every care to ensure the accuracy of our content, mistakes do happen. If you find a mistake in one of our books—maybe a mistake in the text or the code—we would be grateful if you would report this to us. By doing so, you can save other readers from frustration and help us improve subsequent versions of this book. If you find any errata, please report them by visiting `http://www.packtpub.com/submit-errata`, selecting your book, clicking on the **errata submission form** link, and entering the details of your errata. Once your errata are verified, your submission will be accepted and the errata will be uploaded on our website, or added to any list of existing errata, under the Errata section of that title. Any existing errata can be viewed by selecting your title from `http://www.packtpub.com/support`.

Piracy

Piracy of copyright material on the Internet is an ongoing problem across all media. At Packt, we take the protection of our copyright and licenses very seriously. If you come across any illegal copies of our works, in any form, on the Internet, please provide us with the location address or website name immediately so that we can pursue a remedy.

Please contact us at copyright@packtpub.com with a link to the suspected pirated material.

We appreciate your help in protecting our authors, and our ability to bring you valuable content.

Questions

You can contact us at questions@packtpub.com if you are having a problem with any aspect of the book, and we will do our best to address it.

1
Cooking with PhpStorm

In this chapter, we will cover the following recipes:

- ▶ Showing/hiding views
- ▶ Customizing a view
- ▶ Accessing any project file
- ▶ Maximizing views and editors
- ▶ Going back to the previous editor
- ▶ Going back to the previous edit location
- ▶ Linking views to editors
- ▶ Creating a key binding
- ▶ Creating a bookmark
- ▶ Restoring deleted resources
- ▶ Customizing with PhpStorm
- ▶ Adding an include path
- ▶ Excluding unwanted directories from the index
- ▶ Using code completion

Introduction

Finally, your hard work will produce some results—the amount of sweat that you had to perspire to code in PHP will now decrease. The reason behind your being unable to love PHP as a programming language was never trivial. Handling PHP without a strong IDE is no less tough than driving at night with the headlights off. It is always said that PHP is a loosely-typed language (God bless those who say this!), yet PHP errors are nightmarish—with all of those mysterious 500 errors, 403 errors, and the like.

But let us not forget that the error code definitely has a meaning. The Apache server is unable to interpret PHP as such, so it gives you an indication that probably the homework is incomplete and that you have to look into your PHP code and find the exact error yourself. You are left adrift in a leaky boat in a stormy ocean... sad!

To be able to come out of this stormy ocean with a leaky boat, you definitely need some aid: a patch, maybe some better material in the form of a good editor with some really smart intelligence; such intelligence will not only inform you about the error, but also help you a great deal in solving the problem. In short, you need a smart IDE, such as PhpStorm, to code in PHP just as the other creatures in the world of programming do.

PhpStorm understands that programmers are not robots, and thus it leaves no stone unturned in making coding easier for them—be it the beautiful syntax highlighting, code formatting, language injection, error inspection, bookmarking lines of code, and all possible permutations and combinations of the thoughts that are currently coming to your mind. Yes, PhpStorm has a solution to all your coding woes, and it ensures that you can love PHP.

PhpStorm is created and maintained by **JetBrains**, an organization with many similar products in other languages as well. The people at JetBrains respect every community of programmers, and hence they provide IDEs to many programming languages, including Java. PhpStorm is built using the Java programming language and has been carefully designed to be able to support almost all the common and uncommon tools that directly or indirectly provide assistance in programming.

 PhpStorm is an intelligent code editor that provides smart code completion, syntax highlighting, extended code formatting configuration, on-the-fly error checking, code folding, support for language mixtures, and so on.

Showing/hiding views

A **view**, as the name suggests, is a visual area in PhpStorm that enables you, the PHP programmer, to see the various aspects and/or perspectives of the code.

This includes the following:

- The structure of the code you toiled for
- Your favorites (or quick view shortcuts)
- The future plans in the form of a TODO list
- A bird's-eye view of your entire PHP project
- How the code changes in the local system and/or the subversioning system

How to do it...

Perform the following steps:

1. Views in PhpStorm can be shown/hidden via the following keyboard shortcuts and some navigation menu items as well as via some mouse clicks:

Views	Shortcuts
Terminal view	*Alt + F12*
TODO view	*Alt + 6*
Project view	*Alt + 1*
Favorites view	*Alt + 2*
Structure view	*Alt + 7*

2. The best shortcut to access these features is located in the bottom-left corner in PhpStorm and is depicted in the following screenshot:

How it works...

Let us serve the views one at a time so that they can be served hot:

- ▶ **The Terminal view**: PhpStorm ensures that you don't leave it for any reason whatsoever. In case you wish to do some command-line activity, such as running some shell commands, setting some cron jobs or whatever, there is this command terminal available inside PhpStorm. Please remember the keyboard shortcut *Alt + F12*.

- ▶ **The TODO view**: To live the life of a programmer, you need to have multiple core processors to be time-bound; infinite cloud storage volume so that whatever is said to you is recorded somewhere eternally; and 32 GB of RAM so that no context switch pushes the active process out of the memory onto the disk. In short, you need to be Jarvis (Iron Man series). Wake up! You are still a human being with a natural tendency to start dreaming and hence stray from the main topic and forget the main course.

A TODO view in the PhpStorm IDE is a feature with which you can record your future plans to make changes in the code. This not only helps you (in most cases) to remember your plans but also to search for them later when required. A TODO feature is just a sticky note that has literally occupied all the space on your workbench. *Alt + 6* in your sticky note, please.

▶ **The Project view**: A project is analogous to a mechanic's workshop, where great things are made in a not-so-great-looking way. Your project contains all sorts of commented-out code, sample logics, test logics, and failed algorithms, which definitely make you smile at the end of the day when you turn off your computer and go home. In PhpStorm, the Project view is a hierarchical view that shows you the exact hierarchy your code has and what files are located at which node in the tree. In order to show the Project view, use *Alt + 1*.

▶ **The Favorites view**: A favorite is an item or a list that you need quite frequently, so PhpStorm has provided a feature with which you can very easily look up those items. By default, PhpStorm provides three favorites: the bookmarks in your code, the debugger breakpoints in your code that you might have set, and a list containing other favorite items with the same name as you create your project in PhpStorm. The keyboard shortcut is *Alt + 2*.

▶ **The Structure view**: What is more relieving to the mind and the soul than to see the entire code in a consolidated format? The PhpStorm IDE provides a Structure view for code in such a way that all the methods are shown in the form of a list. This enables you to have greater control over the members of any class that you created and prevents namespace collision and method duplication. In order to open the Structure view, all you need to remember is the keyboard shortcut *Alt + 7*.

▶ **The Database view**: Although programming a database is one of the most daunting tasks in the world of programming, PhpStorm eases off this pressure by adding a Database view to the system. It lets you view the database tables, the procedures stored in it, the data stored in it, and a number of general tasks related to databases, which would otherwise have required a dedicated application of its own. The database views can be shown or hidden by simple mouse clicks, as shown in the following recipes. You have the freedom to choose the database server of your choice—it could be a server running on your local system or something running over in the cloud over an IP address and protected by a username and password.

Customizing a view

There are times in the life of a software engineer when nothing seems to be going right, and hence the only thought that comes to mind is to change everything.

PhpStorm takes care of that time period as well and provides customization to the views—you can customize the way views appear.

How to do it...

There are two roads that can take you to the world of customization:

 ► The **Settings** button available in the top-right corner of the individual view, as shown in the following screenshot:

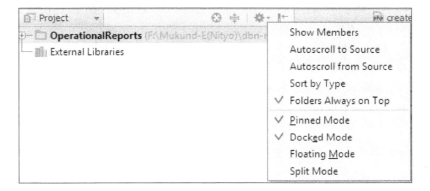

 ► The other very easy option and the most familiar friend of yours is the right-click context menu on the title bar of the toolbar.

How it works...

In general, there are some context menu options available to all the views, such as the orientation modes: floating, docked, pinned, and split. The views can be in:

 ► **Floating Mode**: The views are free to be located anywhere on the screen

 ► **Docked Mode**: The views do not disappear automatically on losing focus

 ► **Pinned Mode**: The view stays at one location until changed

 ► **Split Mode**: You can have multiple views shown at a time

The **Show View as Tabs** option lets you filter or group your tasks based on various criteria, such as project-based, currently-being-edited-based, and scope-based. The **Move** menu allows you to move the view to the top, right, left, or bottom depending upon the current orientation of the view. There are options to stretch or squeeze the view of a window to increase / decrease the size of the view window. The keyboard shortcut is *Ctrl + Shift + Up / Ctrl + Shift + Down* to increase/decrease the size.

There are individual options available for the views. Stay awake to explore customizations of individual view windows, as shown in the following list:

▶ **Terminal View**: More terminal windows can be opened depending on your requirements by clicking on the **+** symbol provided with the Terminal view. If you feel that you need to close the active terminal window, you can very easily do so by clicking on the - symbol on the left-hand side. The commands available for the underlying operating system work fine in this terminal; for example, Linux users can type *Ctrl + D* to exit the terminal, and Windows users can type in their favorite command `dir` in this terminal.

▶ **TODO View**: The special menu options available for this view are listed here:

  ❑ **Select Next Tab**: This shows the next available view inside the TODO view.

  ❑ **Select Previous Tab**: This is used to switch back to the previous view.

  ❑ **Show List of Tabs**: This shows all views. This provides a dropdown to select from the list of available views inside the TODO view, as shown in the following screenshot:

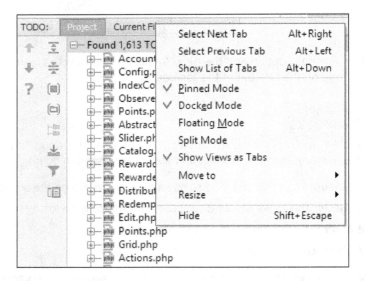

▶ **Project View**: If you are in the **Project View** window, you again deserve more than the general options available. The options are described here. Stay tuned and read on.

  ❑ **Select Next View**: Use this option to go to the next view tab.

  ❑ **Select Previous View**; Use this option to go to the previous view tab.

  ❑ **Show List of Views**: Use this option to select from the list of available views for this window.

- ❑ **Show Members**: If you put a tick mark here, you will be able to see the member functions and variables in the file or code.

- ❑ **Autoscroll to Source**: This option enables a very useful feature. If you select a file here, the same file will be automatically opened in the editor.

- ❑ **Autoscroll from Source**: This is a feature similar to the immediately preceding option. If you select a file in the editor, the Project view will automatically show the same file selected in the Project view.

- ❑ **Sort by Type**: This feature, though seemingly trivial, might prove to be very useful in organizing the files and folders in the project currently being worked upon.

- ❑ **Folders Always on Top**: You can use this feature to let the folders bubble upwards, and the files are automatically shown under the list of folders.

The following screenshot shows how the Project view looks:

- ▶ **Favorites View**: This view section provides three special features:
  - ❑ **Show Members**: This feature shows the list of members in the selected favorite
  - ❑ **Autoscroll from Source**: This is similar to the Project view
  - ❑ **Autoscroll to Source**: This is similar to the Project view

The **Favorites** view is as shown in the following screenshot:

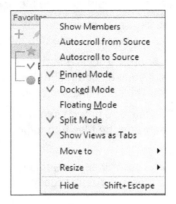

▶ **Structure View**: All you enthusiastic programmers out there should make a habit of using this feature intensively because this is more of an engineering practice than a PHP principle. You should always keep this feature handy, as it definitely is your savior at those times when you feel lost in your hard-labored project. So check your seatbelt, and get ready for this informative ride:

- ❑ **Sort by Visibilit**y: Use this feature to sort your files and folders according to the visibility of the member functions and variables.

- ❑ **Sort Alphabetically**: Friends, remember that this feature will be useful and helpful only in cases where naming conventions have been followed by the rule book. This feature enables the sorting of member functions and variables alphabetically. A descriptive name for the feature, isn't it?

- ❑ **Show Includes**: This feature shows the files included or required programmatically through PHP code as well.

- ❑ **Show Fields**: This feature show the fields in the class/file.

- ❑ **Show Constants**: This feature shows the constant values in the class/file.

- ❑ **Show Inherited**: This feature shows those files/classes that have an inheritance relationship as well.

- ❑ **Show Toolbar**: This feature shows the discussed features in the form of quick access buttons, as shown in the following screenshot:

▶ **Database View**: Most PHP programmers might ask—why do I need to have the Database view in PhpStorm? There should have been something like an SQLStorm for SQL databases.

The reason is related to usability. SQL inside PhpStorm is added just to make everything accessible under one roof and stop the programmer from switching back and forth between PhpStorm and SQLStorm. The right-click context menu options available for this feature are:

❑ **Flatten Schemas**: This feature show the database schema in a rather flattened way rather than in a tree structure.

❑ **Group Tables by Type**: This feature groups the tables by their type. This helps in searching for a table in the database and enhances the viewing of the tables.

❑ **Sort Columns**: This feature sorts columns by name for the database selected.

The **Database** view options are as shown in the following screenshot:

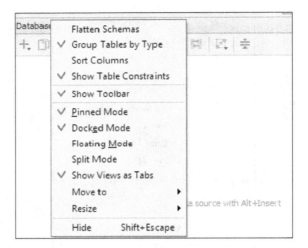

Accessing any project file

Software engineering, at times, becomes more about adjustments than creation. There are practical cases where the developer has no option but to switch to some other project created earlier and now wants to use some feature (without infringing the copyrights and without running the gauntlet of legal action).

Getting ready

If you need to access any project file in PhpStorm, a few decisions can be made. Accessing the project is more important when you handle multiple projects at a time.

How to do it...

If you vaguely remember some of the content that was in the file, you can do a project-wide search to find the target file. Does it make you think of the old story of searching for a needle in a haystack?

1. You can open a folder where your project is supposedly located, as shown in the following screenshot. You can initiate the process by navigating to **File | Open**.

How it works...

Don't worry even if the folder is not a PhpStorm project. PhpStorm is smart enough to manage that. Once opened, the project can be searched for the desired file/resource. PhpStorm will remember the folder as a project, and once indexed, the files of that folder can be accessed just as your current project files.

You have a hotkey at your disposal for the purpose: Try *Ctrl + Shift + N* in times of need, and type in some letters to get a hint list of filenames matching your typed string.

Maximizing views and editors

Although the IT industry is flourishing, and candidates from all across the globe are making a living by IT jobs as programmers, companies continue to be misers in the area of providing infrastructure and maintaining proper ergonomics for the programmers. A small monitor is one such ergonomic infrastructure problem. PhpStorm comes to the rescue.

There is a feature to maximize a view or editor at will. The views can be maximized (when in the docked mode) by the resize option available in the right-click context menu or in the settings menu. For easier handling, the mouse drag can also be handy. Just click and drag the required window to resize.

Good practice says that an editor should be the only object that should be kept visible at all times. The other views should be opened on demand and closed as soon as the task is done. The undocked mode is meant for this purpose. The view appears on demand and disappears as soon as another view or editor is clicked on.

There is an excellent feature available with PhpStorm that lets you concentrate solely on your coding by providing a fullscreen mode, which shows you only the PhpStorm window. Yes, you got it right. Only the PhpStorm window is visible, and no frame border or operating system items are visible.

How to do it...

To turn on this feature, you need to perform the following steps:

1. Go to **View** | **Enter Full Screen**.
2. To turn off, go to **View** | **Exit Full Screen**. Wasn't that easy? Indeed.

An even better feature provided by PhpStorm is the presentation mode. In this, you will only view the editor window with the fonts enlarged. All other features will be available, but only on demand. This is the best viewing option that can be provided by an IDE to work with small or single monitors. Although the motive behind this was to help the programmer demonstrate some coding to an audience, the usage stated in this section is also useful. To turn on this feature, go to **View** | **Enter Presentation Mode**, and to turn off, go to **View** | **Exit Presentation Mode**.

Going back to the previous editor

It is strongly advised that humans only perform one task at a time. This is said because (most) humans cannot multitask, and hence if they attempt to do so, they make mistakes. The same is the case with you, dear.

Getting ready

In the event that you have to work on a project that demands you modify a number of files at once, there is a big chance that you might forget which editor you came from and where to go if the current file being scanned is not the correct copy.

How to do it...

In PhpStorm, you can go back to the previous editor / next editor / choose from the list of open editors by remembering (and obviously using) keymaps. To do so, perform the following steps:

1. Use *Alt + Left* for previous editor.
2. If you want to move to the next editor, use *Alt + Right*.

There's more...

A facility that allows you to move to any part of the code or any class in the open project is available in PhpStorm. This facility enables you to access at random any part of any class or any part of any file that is open in the currently open project, as shown in the following screenshot:

And, as usual, there are some customizations involved in the behavior of PhpStorm. There is a filter symbol. Clicking on the filter symbol, quite implicitly, allows you to filter the search criteria. You can tell PhpStorm not to look in a certain file or resource type by simply unchecking the unwanted file or resource type. Refer to the preceding screenshot for clarity.

To enable random access, every item needs to be added to the index. You can now give credit to the PhpStorm development team for developing this powerful indexing system.

Going back to the previous edit location

You can not only switch between the currently opened editors, but also navigate to the last file you made changes to.

Getting ready

This is particularly helpful in all those cases where you seem to be lost in the load of work that your manager has assigned to you and who wants it to be done in a very short span of time. All programmers in the world have many of the same woes and worries.

How to do it...

In order to access the previous edit location(s), use *Ctrl + Shift + E*, and select the desired file from the list shown in the pop up. It is pretty easy to understand how it works. Let's see a screenshot explaining how to go to the previous editor:

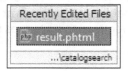

Linking views to editors

Sometimes, the name is self-explanatory. Sometimes, the sentences have a hint. If you got the hint, you must have understood that this feature provided by PhpStorm is intended to show you exactly where in the project heirarchy the code is. If you did not get the hint, don't worry—you've now got it since you've read the text. Please stay tuned for more tasty recipes.

PhpStorm provides two ways of linking between view and editor. PhpStorm can highlight the location of the file you are currently editing in the project tree hierarchy shown in the Project view.

How to do it...

PhpStorm can also open the file in the editor as soon as you select it in the Project view. Perform the following steps:

1. To use this feature, you are advised to read the explanation of *Autoscroll to Source* given in the *Customizing a view* recipe of this chapter.

2. This linking system also applies to the class members (the functions and variables) as well. PhpStorm can autoscroll (or link) between the editor and the view and hence ease some of the pressure of development from your shoulders. So brotherly!

Creating a key binding

For all those people who find key bindings difficult to visualize, key bindings mean keyboard shortcuts, and they are the gear changers in a programmer's life. When you are concentrating hard on the project that you have to complete within a stipulated amount of time, you can bet anything in this world for a way or a means by which your speed of working gets affected positively. Bet on keyboard shortcuts. You will be on the winning side.

PhpStorm, again, specifies some default **keymap** shortcuts. Don't worry friends! You can very easily customize the keyboard shortcuts to suit your taste.

How to do it...

1. Use the keyboard shortcut *Ctrl + Alt + S* or choose from the **File** menu.

2. Go to the **Settings** dialog box and type `keymap` in the search box provided at the top and PhpStorm will highlight the target for you.

3. Choose from a list of the default keymap settings, as shown in the following screenshot, but better late than never. Before jumping to change the shortcuts, understand how shortcuts work in PhpStorm. The keymap shortcuts provided by PhpStorm by default are not directly editable, so in order to customize them, you need to make a copy of the default settings. Sounds confusing? The PhpStorm wizard creates the copy for you. Your mind prompts a question—where are my settings saved then? Here comes the answer—under `*nix` based systems.

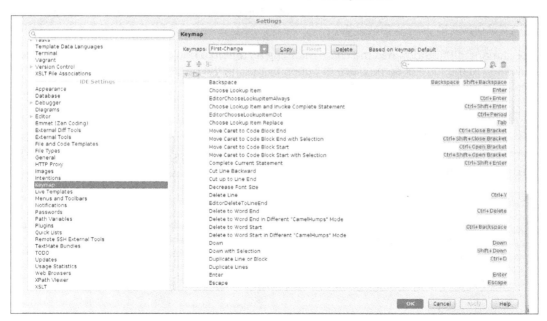

How it works...

PhpStorm uses the directory `~/.WebIde70/config/keymaps` to store all the keymap schemes that you create. Still not feeling confident? Here are the tricks of the trade.

PhpStorm will copy it for you. It will ask you for a name for this keymap scheme. The name you specify will be respected by PhpStorm. A careful observation would easily tell you that PhpStorm will always make you remember that your current selection is based on the setting provided by PhpStorm. After you have made the selection to copy and modify, all you have to do is to press the **Apply** button. Bingo! You just created a copy of one default setting, and now you are all set to customize PhpStorm behavior your own way.

To verify that, you can go to `~/.WebIde70/config/keymaps` and see that PhpStorm just created a new XML file for you that contains the settings you created via the PhpStorm GUI. Behind every successful frontend, there is an equally strong backend!

If you think that you can speak XML, you can create some settings via the GUI and then view the contents of the XML file to observe how the settings are saved. You can later add items directly to the XML file. You naughty hacker! Control your smile!

Creating a bookmark

Bookmarks are great. A bookmark lets you put a flag somewhere in your code so that you have a shortcut to access that code.

A bookmark in PhpStorm has the same meaning as that in a book where a reader puts some indication in the form of some piece of paper, by turning the page corner, or by any means through which the reader can access the page directly.

How to do it...

PhpStorm bookmarks are created with ease. The add bookmark option can be had by going to **Navigate | Bookmarks**.

The three options available are explained here:

▶ **Toggle Bookmark**: This feature enables you to create a bookmark at some specified line of code if it does not exist and to delete a bookmark from some line of code if it does.

▸ **Toggle Bookmark with Mnemonic**: This feature enables you to toggle a bookmark with the added ability to be able to access that bookmark using keyboard shortcuts.

Suppose you choose the alphanumeric **0**, as shown in the following screenshot, you will be able to access that bookmark by using *Ctrl + 0*

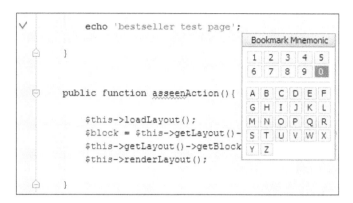

Show Bookmarks: This is rather a simple feature. It simply lets you view all the bookmarks you created for the project you are working on.

Quick access to bookmark

In order to have quick access to the bookmark feature with the mnemonic feature, all the hard work that you have to do is remember the keyboard shortcut *Ctrl + F11*. The rest will be taken care of by PhpStorm automatically.

Restoring deleted resources

To err is human. To recover from the error cleanly is PhpStorm. It is perfectly okay for you to commit mistakes. You could be thinking of your ex or your reporting manager's atrocities on you to make you work overtime (while he himself keeps tinkering with social networking sites), and you happen to accidentally delete some lines from your code. You have no idea what you did, and with a heavy heart, you went home at the close of day. The very next morning, when you are about to start work, you suddenly realize that you deleted some lines of code and you don't remember which! Is this something like salt on burnt skin? Need ointment? Breathe and thank PhpStorm's team of developers who knew that you are a human prone to making drastic mistakes like these.

Getting ready

You can recover the lines deleted from your code. Yes, you got that right. There is the history feature in PhpStorm that is one of the best in its class in terms of the visual assistance it provides in finding the change that has occurred to your code—be it local, that is, you were the culprit behind the notorious code change, be it from the team, that is, someone else's code ruined yours. PhpStorm helps you point out the mistake or error and helps you in fixing things quickly.

How to do it...

PhpStorm keeps a snapshot of every code that you write. It updates it every time you save. So, if you need to undelete a piece of code, you need to dive into the history using the times of editing the files as anchors. As soon as you change to another window it automatically saves the document...wasn't that cool. Perform the following steps:

1. The **Local History** option is available on the mouse right-click context menu.

2. As soon as you click on or select a particular time, PhpStorm shows you the difference between that file from history and your current file, as shown in the following screenshot:

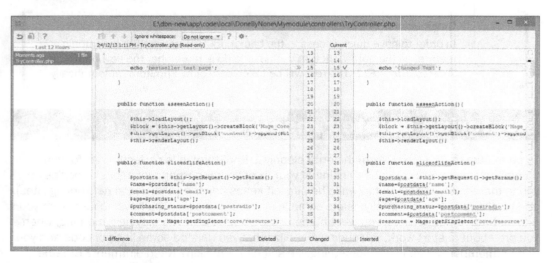

3. You can revert to (this) particular item by selecting the **Revert** option from the right-click context menu. Done!

4. You can also merge the code line by line by double-clicking on the greater-than sign (**>>**).

How it works...

If you deleted a file from PhpStorm, knowingly or unknowingly, you can use the same feature to recover your deleted files. You need to select the target folder or directory from the Project view, access the right-click context menu, and select the **Local History | Show History** option. PhpStorm will not only show you all the files that you deleted very easily, but also in a hierarchical way, as shown in the following screenshot:

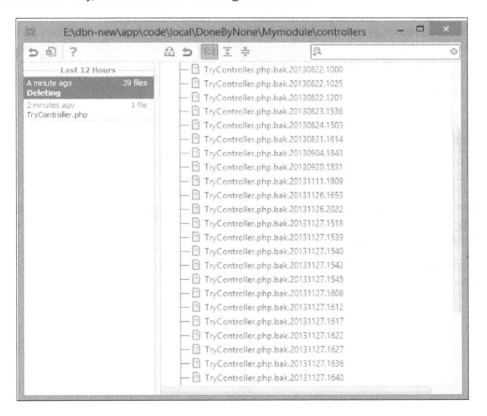

All you need to do is to access the right-click context menu on the file that you want to recover from the list and choose the **Revert Selection** option. No more cigarettes and coffee combinations, please. Your headache is solved.

Customizing with PhpStorm

Sometimes thinking enough is not enough. Sometimes doing enough is not enough. The point is, despite learning so much, you still have a feeling that some more customization could have been possible. PhpStorm is at your disposal.

Getting ready

The best thing you can do is use PhpStorm for whatever PHP projects you take up. But therein the problem looms large. Executing PHP via a web server is OK, but what do you do about the use case when the script has to run in the background? What if your reporting manager wants you to do some socket programming? You need a command-line interpreter for PHP. Stunned silence? It's time to break that silence. Thank PhpStorm and integrate the command-line PHP interpreter with PhpStorm.

How to do it...

Just a small sequence of shortcuts is all that you need to invoke command-line PHP. There are actually two roads, that is, there is a bifurcation ahead. From the bifurcation, you will see two roads—on the left-hand side is the *PhpStormish* way, and on the right-hand side is the *operating systemish* way. The point worth noting is that both ways take you to the same destination. At the destination, you will attain your goal, which is to have the capacity to use PhpStorm for every PHP task.

You will be taken through the PhpStormish way first. This is easier, so you should try it first. This is termed as PhpStormish because PhpStorm lets you think that you are using PhpStorm itself to run your hard toiled PHP code. Perform the following steps:

1. In order to run command-line PHP this way, you need to go to **Settings | PHP**, as shown in the next screenshot:

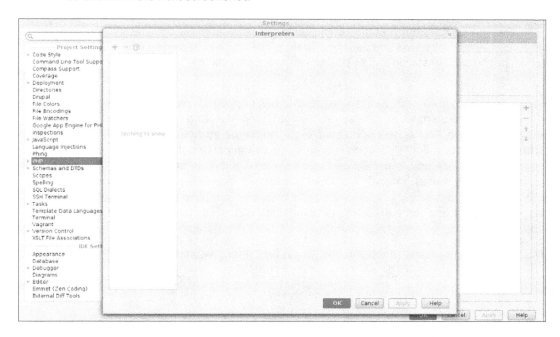

2. There is this interpreter dropdown. You need to add an interpreter. You can do that by selecting the PHP interpreter from the `bin` folder of the PHP installation.

3. Once selected, you need to customize it by providing various parameters, such as a name and configuration options. On applying the changes, the PHP environment in PhpStorm will be powered by the PHP environment of your underlying operating system.

4. This will enable you to test and run your PHP scripts using the default keyboard shortcut *Ctrl + Shift + F10*.

See also

 You can add more interpreters if you have multiple versions of PHP installed and select from those for execution.

That was easy to cook, right? Feeling happy? In this happiness, please don't forget that there was one more road, which was on the right-hand side, and which again took us to the same destination. PHP scripts or codes can be run on the terminal. Terminal—did this word strike bells in your mind? PhpStorm provides you a terminal (emulator) such that you do not have to switch back and forth between your beloved IDE (presumably) PhpStorm and the command-line terminal. You can again use this feature to execute command-line PHP scripts. All you have to do is type `php your-php-file.php` if you have the PHP classpath set, or else you need to add some extra letters to make it `/path/to/installed-php/php your-php-file.php`.

The following screenshot shows you how to run PHP through command line in PhpStorm:

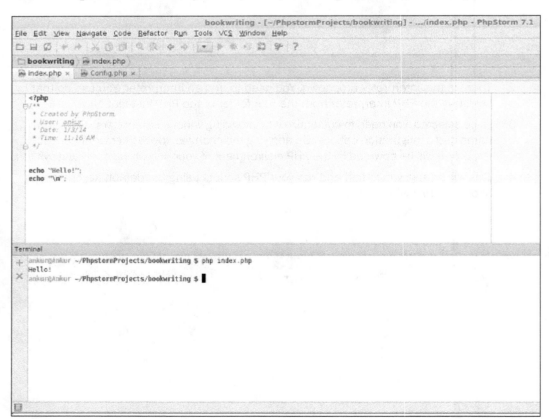

Adding an include path

One of the software engineering principles says that components should be reusable, that is, the structure of the software should be modular. This is a practice accepted worldwide, but this adds an overhead to the translation (interpreter or compiler) to link the modules together by first finding them. PHP is no different.

Getting ready

The PHP interpreter has to search for the required files/folders/resources every time the script is run. PhpStorm can, however, decrease the time required to search for the files/folders by allowing you to set the include path. The include path is the base directory under your operating system that contains all the files and folders to the dependencies.

How to do it...

You have the freedom to set this in PhpStorm. Go to **Settings | PHP | Include Path**. Select the new path. Click on **Apply**. Done! Take a look at the following screenshot, which illlustrates this point:

You should always make sure that you plan how to organize your files and folders beforehand so that a minimum number of include path settings are required.

If a folder is provided in the include path, it will be helpful in autocompletion for `include()`, `require()`, and so on.

Excluding unwanted directories from the index

Did you try imagining why on earth PhpStorm has information about all the files you added in your project directory structure? How does PhpStorm detect the changes that you make to the disk by adding images, text files, and so on, and manages to show them in the Project view? Yes, the answer is indexing.

Getting ready

PhpStorm indexes everything that comes its way. Thus, it remembers the files and folders properly. But there is an overhead involved in this system. The more the number of files in the project, the longer the index created is. If PhpStorm decreases time in searching for files and folders by maintaining an index, how will it manage searching in the index itself when the index list has increased to a very large size?

How to do it...

You can help PhpStorm by performing the following steps:

1. Go to **Settings | Directories**.
2. Select a directory, and all you have to remember from here are three keyboard shortcuts: *Alt + T*, *Alt + E*, and *Alt + R*. Consider the following screenshots:

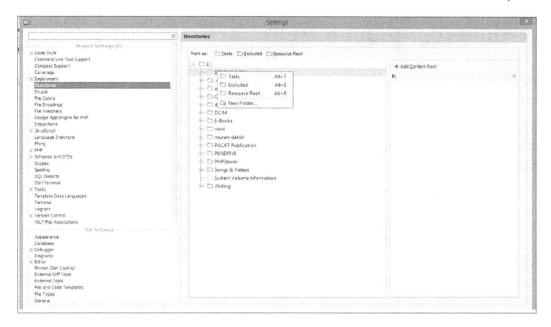

How it works...

Alt + T will mark a resource as a test resource, *E* will exclude it from indexing, and *R* will mark it as the content root. For you, the increase in speed will come from the magic key combination *Alt + E*. Be ruthless enough to apply this magic to all those directories that you decide are not important enough to be indexed.

A test resource is a type of resource, most probably some PHP script, some directory, or some other file type that is used in the testing process. So, you can mark a resource as a test resource once you know that it will be useful for testing purposes.

PhpStorm, being a careful(ly written) piece of software, maintains a list of all the files that you save in your project, using indexes. So, a large number of files means a longer index and hence the potential danger of slowing PhpStorm down. An excluded resource is a resource—some file(s) or folder(s)—that you have asked PhpStorm not to index.

A content root is a folder or directory under which the contents of the resources you are working on is contained. You would easily be tempted to ask "what purpose does it serve?" The answer is rather simple: it maintains a clean workspace for you (everything in life need not be complicated)!

Using code completion

The best example of the need to use an IDE instead of a standard editor is that an IDE understands your code and thus provides hints about the code that you might be writing or need next.

Getting ready

A standard editor would, at the maximum, provide basic text coloring based on the various keywords. Anyway, without hurting the feelings of editors, PhpStorm provides you with additional options besides providing you the standard code completion system.

How to do it...

There is the smart type completion that not only completes your code, but also finds and suggests the most eligible match for your code. By eligible, it means that the code hint matches the current context (the invoking object). This is particularly useful in cases in which you have honestly stuck to the *Software Engineering principle of Inheritance*.

Code completion settings in PhpStorm are available at **File | Settings | Editor | Code Completion**, as shown in the following screenshot:

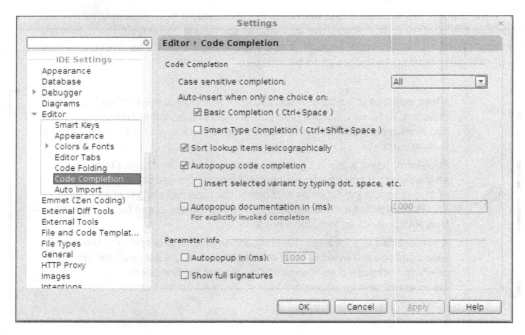

How it works...

If you have a lot of items for PhpStorm to look up, for example, members of your created class, you can order PhpStorm to provide you with hints in lexicographical order.

To turn this feature on, you need to select the checkbox adjacent to **Sort lookup items lexicographically**. The following screenshot shows the code completion feature:

```
\Controllers\BookWriting
<?php
/** Created by PhpStorm. ...*/

namespace Controllers;


class BookWriting {
    function __construct(){

    }

    public function_
}
```

__clone()	mixed
__construct()	void
__destruct()	void
__get(name : string)	mixed
__invoke()	mixed
__isset(name : string)	bool
__set(name : string, value)	void
__set_state(an_array : array)	mixed
__sleep()	array|NULL
__toString()	string

Dot, semicolon and some other keys will also close this lookup and be inserted into editor

Code completion at your convenience! I hope this make sense to you.

2
PHP Development

In this chapter, we will cover the following topics:

- ► Creating a PHP project using Composer
- ► Creating an empty project
- ► Reusing an existing project
- ► Creating a new PHP class
- ► Creating a new PHP method
- ► Adding the getter/setter methods
- ► Creating delegate methods
- ► Surrounding code with control structures
- ► Finding the matching brace
- ► Commenting out a section of code and PHPDoc
- ► Creating a working set
- ► Creating TODO tasks

Introduction

Now that you have your headlights turned on, you can have that "come what may" attitude and set out to drive your favorite car—PHP. Go ahead and give it your best shot now that you have your beloved tool ready—PhpStorm. PhpStorm will take care of eliminating the distractions from your life and will let you concentrate on programming.

You can think of any aspect in solving a problem using PHP, and PhpStorm will be there to assist you.

Do you have an imminent problem to solve, some problem that appears daunting to you, or some problem that has challenged your existence as a software engineer? If you stick to the software engineering principles, PhpStorm will leverage your capacity and let you do wonders while solving the problems at hand. PhpStorm lets you focus on designing your business logic by offloading you from the worries of remembering the finer details, such as the exact method signature and the list of parameters.

Imagine that you have been called by your manager to discuss some new feature for the business that has to be developed in, as usual, no time at all. You are again in a fix. That decision to choose between the devil and the deep blue sea again looms large.

PhpStorm users need not worry. They have a third option—to board a helicopter and reach their destination from the current scenario.

You were brave enough to gather the requirements from the business end. Which way do you chose now? Decide whether you want to go right or left. If you go to the right, you will take the route to create a new project. If you go to the left, you will take the route to reuse an existing project and make modifications in it.

Wherever you go and whichever road you take, you have to reach the same destination. In the end, you have to report to your manager what you did to achieve the target. Not only do you have to decide quickly, but you also have to act swiftly.

Creating a PHP project using Composer

Welcome to those who have taken the route to the right! Fasten your seatbelts, and get ready to create a new project in PHP.

Creating a new project in itself is a very mature decision, so you should always decide maturely and strategically. There might be situations in which, out of sheer enthusiasm, you opted to create a new project, and within a few days, you realize that much of the functionality you are planning to create has already been developed. You will end up doing a lot of copy-pasting work.

Getting ready

The principles of software engineering always teach students that a design should be high on coupling and low on cohesion. This means that an application program should use other programs but not depend on it. Composer in PHP is a system that helps you to adopt this methodology. Composer is a dependency manager for PHP, which allows other packages written in PHP to be included in other projects.

PhpStorm enables you to create projects that adhere to this principle. To create a new Composer project, you need to select the **Composer Project** option in the dropdown provided from the **File** | **New Project** menu item. The next question asked of you is to select the path of `composer.phar`—from the local disk or from the website: `http://www.getcomposer.org`

How to do it...

Don't scratch your head out of utter confusion—more knowledge surely means more confusion, but that never means you should target zero knowledge to have no confusion at all! An executable, `composer.phar`, causes this magic of handling the packages to occur. You must be thinking what exactly is it inside Composer that makes it such a buzzword these days—everyone seems to be talking about it. Perform the following steps:

1. Go to `https://getcomposer.org/download/`, and you will see that there is the following command:

    ```
    curl -sS https://getcomposer.org/installer | php
    ```

2. If you have already installed composer prior to coming to cook with PhpStorm, you should specify `/path/to/composer.phar`, the path to where composer has been installed.

3. You can then select from the list of available packages in the left-hand side panel. On the right, you can see the corresponding description of the package selected. You can select the version of the package to be installed, and then click on **OK**.

Downloading the example code

You can download the example code files for all Packt books you have purchased from your account at `http://www.packtpub.com`. If you purchased this book elsewhere, you can visit `http://www.packtpub.com/support` and register to have the files e-mailed directly to you.

How it works...

The command is actually a concatenation of two commands that get the contents of the installer script and execute that via the PHP command line. If you happen to open the specified link inside a web browser, you will see the entire PHP code behind Composer. Are you able to breathe freely (pun intended)? Back to work, the intention of the second part of the command is to execute the PHP content via the PHP command line.

Backtracking to the original topic, you were trying to select the right type of `composer.phar`. Have a look at the following screenshot:

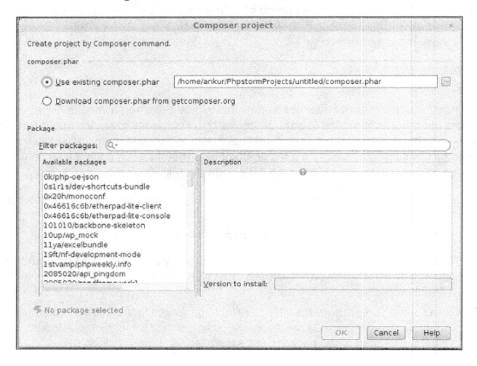

PhpStorm takes care of the remaining tasks in installing *your-selected-package*.

The Composer system generates a `json` file with the name `composer.json`, which contains the details about the requirements. The following is the `composer.json` file for a project that has been created from scratch:

```
{
  "name": "2085020/api_pingdom",
  "description": "pingdom api for php",
  "require": {
    "guzzle/guzzle": "v2.7.2"
  },
  "authors": [
    {
      "name": "Emagister",
      "email": "jcruz@emagister.com"
    }
  ],
  "autoload": {
    "psr-0": {
```

```
        "Emagister":"src"
    }
  }

}
```

It is quite apparent that the json file conveys a lot of information to the reader. `"name"`: is the name of the package downloaded. `"description"`: is the description of the package downloaded. If you have a good memory, you will remember that there was a description in the right-hand panel of the package selection window. This description is exactly the same. `"require"`: is the name of the packages that this downloaded package depends upon. The json file specifies the name of the project as the key and the corresponding version number as the value. `"authors"`: is the author of the downloaded package. It includes the name and e-mail address of the author. `"autoload"`: is the coding standard, any of PSR-0, PSR-1, PSR-2, PSR-3, PSR-4, and the namespace mapping to the actual directory. The hierarchy goes like this: the coding-standard contains the value of the namespace mapping. Namespace mapping means the name as the key and the directory (relative to the project root) as the value.

PhpStorm and the Composer combination work wonders. When you order PhpStorm to download and arrange the packages, it will automatically arrange for you the include paths for the projects. No more warnings or errors relating to missing files will present a hindrance to your work now. Consider the following sreenshot:

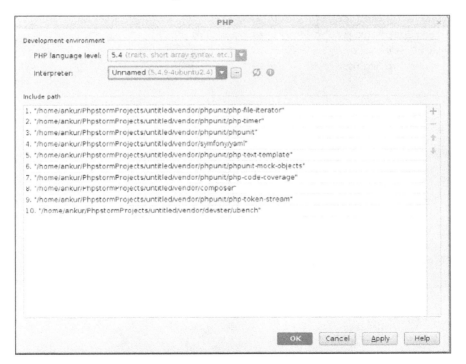

Suppose you have already added a few packages in your project and you now realize that you need to have more of the packages. Not to worry says PhpStorm, as it provides you an option to add more packages in the form of **Add dependency**. Doing this is extremely easy. In the open project, you need to go to **Tools | Composer | Add dependency**. There will be a familiar pop up that will ask you to select a package name and proceed to install. The remainder of the tasks will, as usual, be taken care of by PhpStorm. The result you will see will be in the form of some downloaded files and folders besides a change in your composer.json file for this particular project. One such composer.json file is as shown in the following code snippet:

```json
{
    "name": "redis/ranking",
    "description": "Wrapping Redis's sorted set APIs for specializing
ranking operations.",
    "keywords": ["redis", "ranking", "sort", "realtime"],
    "homepage": "https://github.com/matsubo/redis-ranking",
    "type": "library",
    "license": "PHP3",
    "require" : {
      "php": ">=5.3.0",
      "lib/curl": "0.3",
      "php-curl-class/php-curl-class": "1.0.1",
      "php-mod/curl": "1.0",
      "development/curl": "dev-master",
      "phpdocumentor/phpdocumentor": "2.0.0b7",
      "abhi/tangocard": "dev-master",
      "10up/wp_mock": "dev-master"
    },
    "authors": [
      {
        "name": "Yuki Matsukura",
        "email": "matsubokkuri@gmail.com"
      }
    ],


    "require": {
    },
    "require-dev": {
      "devster/ubench": "1.1.*-dev",
      "phpunit/phpunit": "3.*"
    },
    "autoload": {
      "psr-0": {"Matsubo": "src/"}
    }
}
```

The symbols have the usual meaning. The external dependencies have been added to the list according to the json notation and are denoted by the single key required, where the value is the actual list of the dependencies having the key as their name and the corresponding versions as the value.

Creating an empty project

The feeling that you get when you find some support in times of trouble can be said to have an analogy with that feeling of finding cold water to drink in times of thirst. This statement's analogy with the current scenario is that until this point in time, you were unable to find the exact project type to create, but now you have found a way out.

Getting ready

You need to create an empty PHP project when you are convinced enough to need to create a new project and achieve a new feat by fulfilling your manager's business demand.

How to do it...

A new empty project is the easiest to create:

1. You need to specify a name for your new project. Don't worry even if there are spelling mistakes in the name itself because PhpStorm doesn't check the name you specify against the dictionary.

2. A project name should only contain valid characters that a directory name should contain under an operating system.

How it works...

Creating an empty project is easy to understand. You need to specify the /path/to/files/ and/folders/ if you already have some basic framework to start from. See *Integrating Frameworks*, else PhpStorm will manage that for you by setting the default path (~/PhpstormProjects/<name-of-your-project>).

Reusing an existing project

Those who planned to take the route on the right-hand side have rightly chosen to do so. At times, reinventing the wheel is not a wise action to perform.

Getting ready

If you reuse, you will be able to avoid spending time and resources on something that has already been created. PhpStorm allows you to reuse existing projects and lets you move forward. To reuse an existing project, you need to have the project on the disk.

How to do it...

To open an existing project, perform the following steps:

1. You need to go to **File | Open**. There will be a pop-up dialog from PhpStorm.
2. You need to tell PhpStorm the path of the directory where your project is saved, and PhpStorm will obediently open the project for you.

 Once a directory has been opened as a project in PhpStorm, you will be able to distinguish it the next time because PhpStorm puts its logo next to this directory.

You can now concentrate on gathering your technical requirements. You are strongly advised to plan well in advance before actually jumping to code because although a perfect software engineering plan does not exist yet, you can be optimistic and create a good enough plan that is flexible enough to be modified in case of need.

Creating a new PHP class

Having come to the kitchen, you should be prepared to get your hands dirty while cooking. You will have to face the class spills, member variable splashes, and literal wetness of sweat when you try to bake the data structures; they might be too hot to handle. You might end up causing a burning sensation inside you (out of control *acidity*; pun intended). You must be prepared to have mistakenly added less (syntactic) sugar, thought of incorrect salt handling algorithm. All sorts of cooking issues would be there to trouble you, which might make you leave cooking altogether and run away... scary? Maybe yes... but you will not tire, you will not falter, and you will not fail dear friends, Romans and countrymen!

Getting ready

Some fundamentals... some programmers always talk **class**. In fact, all should. If you have always wondered what exactly a class is, you need to understand a datatype first. You must now have started feeling nostalgic, recalling your school days when teachers continued to haunt you with all those alien words. Come back and try to understand what a datatype is.

A **datatype** is a classification of data based on its type (some would like to call this its attribute) and the operations (some prefer calling this its behavior). So what is the relation between class and datatype? The answer is that a class is a custom datatype. Puzzled? Please do not be. If you attempt to create a class, what do you do? You plan a number of member variables... STOP.

What is a variable defined as? There is the connection. So, the complete statement now becomes: you plan a number of member variables, methods (functions, as some prefer saying) to pack inside a class.

A class can be inherited from another class, can implement an interface, or be designed to be inherited. You can think of any permutation from the set {simple, abstract, inherited, super, and sub}, and you will observe that most of the permutations will be valid. How do you attack a problem? Simple common sense would suggest attacking the easiest part of the problem. So, here is how you can create a simple PHP class using PhpStorm.

How to do it...

To be about to create a new class, you might have already created a project. Inside that project, you can create a new class by selecting the target folder and accessing the right-click context menu.

PhpStorm is a curious machine. No sooner do you ask it to do something for you than it starts asking you a number of questions related to it. Here, when you ask PhpStorm to create a new class for you, it will ask you the following:

- ▸ **Name**: This is quite self explanatory and is a mandatory field. You need to tell PhpStorm the name of the class you want to be created. You should be careful while naming your class, as this has to be in sync with your project engineering plan.

- ▸ **Namespace**: This is a handle-with-care option. You need to specify the namespace in order to explicitly tell the interpreter which version of the function to use. This is an optional but important field—if you do not specify it, nothing bad will happen and you will not suffer any illness.

- ▸ **Filename**: This is an option you need to be careful while using. By default, this assumes the same value as the name of the class. If you mishandle this option by providing some other name, any product that you create will be solely owned by destiny, and no engineering principle will be able to maintain your product with ease.

- ▸ **Directory**: Here, you can set the location where you wish your class to physically reside on the disk. By default, it assumes the location where you created your project—project root to be precise.

> ► **Kind**: Now, this is something you have to decide based on the type of engineering plan that you have made prior to selecting this project. If you had a plan according to which you will be able to decide the functionality at a later stage, you can set the type of file as an interface; or for all other cases, you need to select the type as class. This interface is required in those conditions in which you will add the salt to the recipe later (pun intended). A trait is something that has a philosophy of "me too".
> You can safely ignore it for now.

> ► **File extension**: This is an option that you are not advised to unnecessarily change. At the heart of all PHP files lies only one extension—the `.php` file. PhpStorm knows this. Please allow it to proceed.

The add class option is available via two menu items. One has already been discussed, and for the other, perform the following step:

1. Go to **File** | **New**:

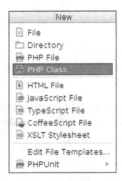

How it works...

A simple sample class would look like the following code snippet:

```php
<?php
class Review {

}
```

Creating an interface in PhpStorm is not difficult either. On telling PhpStorm to create an interface, the output will be similar to a class except that there will be the keyword interface that will replace the keyword class. It will look like the following:

```php
<?php

interface Readable {
```

If you want to differentiate class and interface, then you just need common sense in terms of PHP. A `Class` keyword is used for class and `interface` for creating interfaces in PHP.

Creating a new PHP method

If classes that represent real-world entities are nouns, they do not have any existence without verbs—the actions to be performed. To be able to maximize the technical profit for the manager you work for, you must be ready to use functions for all the verbs that exist in your use case.

Getting ready

Say for example, you have a pizza cooking task at hand. The recipe would consist of a (bare minimum) pizza bread (a noun), cheese (a noun), some salt (a noun). If you ponder over your problem, you will realize that you need to apply cheese to your pizza bread and add salt according to taste. If you look at this scenario from a technical perspective, you would most probably decide that there would be a `PizzaDish` class with functions such as `applyCheese(pizzaBread)`, `addSalt(cheese)`, and so on.

How to do it...

Creating a method in PhpStorm is easy. Suppose you have your `PizzaDish` class. Your pizza dish is a `Dish` so your `PizzaDish` would extend `Dish`. Your class would look like the following code snippet:

```php
<?php
class Dish {
/**
* @param string $dishName The name of the dish
*/
protected function addSalt(){}
}
```

Your `PizzaDish` class can look like the following code snippet:

```php
<?php
class PizzaDish extends Dish{
  private $dishName;
  function addSalt($dishName){
    $this->dishName = $dishName;
    parent::addSalt($this->dishName);
  }
}
```

Coding in PhpStorm is eased heavily by the use of code hinting or code completion. You just need to type a few characters as a hint, and PhpStorm is ready to suggest what could be next. You type `fun` and press *Ctrl + Space*, and there will be a number of hints about what your function can be. If you want to do more with your pizza creation recipe, as in adding some more ingredients, such as capsicum or mushroom, you can have a general function, `add($ingredient, $dishname)`. You can do that in your `PizzaDish` class. You can make use of code completion for the access modifier. You have to manually take care of the other actions.

To convert the method `addSalt()` to `add()`, you need to rename the `addSalt` method. This is done in PhpStorm by the refactor option.

To refactor an item (here, the `addSalt` method), access the right-click context menu | **Refactor** | **Rename** or **Refactor** | **Change Signature**.

The **Rename** submenu, as shown in the following screenshot, will only change the name of the method:

The **Change Signature** option is a more detailed refactoring facility in which you can change the complete signature of a method, as shown in the following screenshot:

So, your new add function becomes like the following code snippet:

```php
<?php
require_once 'Dish.php';

class PizzaDish extends Dish{
  private $dishName;

  function __construct($dishName){
    $this->dishName = $dishName;
  }

  function add($ingredientName){
    parent::add($this->dishName, $ingredientName);
  }
}
```

A similar change has occurred in the parent `Dish` class as well, where the method `addSalt` has been renamed to `add`, as shown in the following code:

```php
<?php
class Dish {
  /**
   * @param string $dishName   The name of the dish
   */
  protected function add($dishName, $ingredient){
  }
}
```

You can make use of the `PizzaDish` class and its methods by firing the code shown in the following screenshot:

```php
$pizzaDish = new PizzaDish('New Pizza');
$pizzaDish->add('salt');
$pizzaDish->add('cheese');
$pizzaDish->add('capsicum');
```

How it works...

The working of the code ecosystem is quite simple. You instantiated the `PizzaDish` class normally. You invoked the `add` function. But, when you actually invoked the `add` function, what exactly happened? The `add` function called the `add` function defined in its parent class (remember extends added to the beginning of `PizzaDish`) using a special word—`parent`. So, you called the `add` method thinking that `PizzaDish` would do your work, but in reality, `Dish` did your work! No, no, this is not cheating. This is inheritance, as explained by the principles of software engineering.

 The keyboard shortcuts are *Ctrl + F6* and *Shift + F6* to change the signature and rename respectively.

Adding the getter/setter methods

Adding `getter` and `setter` methods in PhpStorm is equally easy. All you need to do is have a member variable of the class. In the `PizzaDish` example, it was `dishName`.

Getting ready

To create getters and setters for `dishName`, PhpStorm provides that if you need to. Access the right-click context menu for the target variable, click on **Generate** and select **Getters** and **Setters** from the pop up. PhpStorm will create the desired getters and setters for the selected member.

Your `PizzaDish` class will now look like the following piece of code:

```php
<?php
require_once 'Dish.php';

class PizzaDish extends Dish{
  private $dishName;

  /**
  * @param mixed $dishName
  */
  public function setDishName($dishName)
  {
    $this->dishName = $dishName;
  }

  /**
    * @return mixed
  */
  public function getDishName()
  {
    return $this->dishName;
  }
  function add($ingredientName){
    $this->setDishName($ingredientName);
    parent::add($this->dishName);
  }
}
```

How to do it...

The process of adding salt, cheese, and capsicum is still the same.

You have to send the following lines to your PHP engine in order to create a new pizza dish and add some ingredients to it:

```php
$pizzaDish = new PizzaDish('New Pizza');
$pizzaDish->add('salt');
$pizzaDish->add('cheese');
$pizzaDish->add('capsicum');
```

How it works...

Earlier, when you had to access `$dishName`, you did it directly. This initiated a number of poor engineering practices, such as exposing the representation of the member variables. Actually, the list is endless. All you need to do is ensure that you must use getters and setters to be a good software engineer. So, in the code provided to you, you just have to call the `getter` method (such as `getDishName`) and the `setter` method (such as `setDishName`).

Are you still feeling uncomfortable? Have patience. Welcome to the real software engineering world.

Creating delegate methods

Delegation is an important design pattern in software engineering. It enhances code reusability.

Getting ready

In PHP, delegate methods can be created in accordance with the principle of delegation. While calling delegate functions, you need not know the name of the actual function in advance—the PHP engine can find it out at runtime for you.

How to do it...

PHP provides two factory methods for the purpose. However, you can create your own delegate methods using the principles of **object-oriented programming**.

The factory methods provided by PHP are `call_user_func()` and `call_user_func_array()`. While the usage of the two methods is out of the scope of this text, the creation and usage of the delegate methods is better explained by the same scenario of cooking `PizzaDish`, as shown in the following code:

```php
<?php
require_once 'Dish.php';

class PizzaDish{
  private $dishName;

  /**
    * @param mixed $dishName
    */
  public function setDishName($dishName)
  {
```

```php
    $this->dishName = $dishName;
  }

  /**
   * @return mixed
   */
  public function getDishName()
  {
    return $this->dishName;
  }

  private $instance;

  /**
    * @return mixed
   */
  public function getInstance()
  {
    return $this->instance;
  }


  /**
    * @param mixed $instance
   */
  public function setInstance($instance)
  {
    $this->instance = new $instance;
  }


  function __construct($dishName, $instanceName){
    $this->setInstance($instanceName);
    $this->setDishName($dishName);
  }


  function add($ingredientName){
    $this->getInstance()->add($ingredientName);
  }
}
```

The usage of the delegate method is almost the same, but not the same:

```php
$pizzaDish = new PizzaDish('New Pizza', 'Dish');
$pizzaDish->add('salt');
$pizzaDish->add('cheese');
$pizzaDish->add('capsicum');
```

And the `Dish` class now looks like the following:

```php
<?php
class Dish {
  /**
    * @param string $ingredient The name of the ingredient to be
added
    */
  public function add($ingredient){
    echo "\nYou have added: ", $ingredient;
  }
}
```

How it works...

Surprised? What is happening here is that when you invoke the `PizzaDish` class and pass the name of the `Dish` class in the constructor, the value of `$instance` is a newly created object of the `Dish` class. The rest, as it goes, is the usual method call via a class object. You can take a deep breath now, as you have just delegated the `add` function in `PizzaDish` to use the `add` function of `Dish`. It appears that the `PizzaDish` class is performing the task, but the actual task is done by the `Dish` class.

Surrounding code with control structures

Whatever algorithm you think of, whichever tool you use to design the functional requirements, and whichever planet you go to and use whatever hardware as your development platform, there is this fact that is omnipresent and ubiquitous: loops will follow you everywhere. Control structures are the building blocks of any code you think of. Not convinced? Your `PizzaDish` use case itself will be able to prove it to you.

Getting ready

You need a computer in the first place to make calculations and decisions and solve complex problems in a diligent manner. Does a computer stop by solving just one problem? No. It is programmed to continue for all possible number of times it has been instructed. How does a program achieve this diligence? You said it right. A bit louder please. Yes, control loops. Even though this explanation might appear trivial to all you big guns, yet it is right that you cannot proceed to code without control structures.

PhpStorm lets you write code. It lets you concentrate on the actual business logic. You can write the lines of code that you think would be the atomic part. When you are convinced that the logic fits, you can use PhpStorm's **Surround** with feature to surround this code in your desired control structure.

How to do it...

If you wish to add ingredients to your `PizzaDish`, you can make use of loops. There are multiple ways to express a single statement:

- Using `foreach`, the `PizzaDish` class is invoked as follows:

```php
$pizzaDish = new PizzaDish('New Pizza', 'Dish');
$ingredients = array('salt','cheese','capsicum');
foreach ($ingredients as $ingredient) {
$pizzaDish->add($ingredient);
}
```

  You had to write `$pizzaDish->add($ingredient)` while keeping the cursor on this line.

  Invoke Surround by going to **Code | Surround with**, and selecting the `foreach` option did the trick for you. However, you had to specify the variables inside the loop structure. You can also use the keyboard shortcut *Ctrl + Alt + T*.

- You can perform a similar action for the `for` loop. This change will allow you to invoke your code. Have a look at the following code snippet:

```php
$pizzaDish = new PizzaDish('New Pizza', 'Dish');
$ingredients = array('salt','cheese','capsicum');
for ($count = 0; $count < count($ingredients); $count++) {
  $pizzaDish->add($ingredients[$count]);
}
```

- A similar action is performed by surrounding the code with a `while` control structure. Your `PizzaDish` gets invoked by the following code snippet:

```php
$pizzaDish = new PizzaDish('New Pizza', 'Dish');
$ingredients = array('salt', 'cheese', 'capsicum');
$ingredientCount = 0;
while ($ingredientCount < count($ingredients)) {
  $pizzaDish->add($ingredients[$ingredientCount]);
$ingredientCount++;
}
```

A careful observation will reveal that the `while` loop behavior is exactly the same as the `for` loop behavior. Why have two features to achieve the same functionality, then? The human mind feels happy on having more choices. A piece of (pseudo) code explains this better:

```php
while($moreChoicesAvailable){
  $humanMind = array(
    'feeling' => 'happy',
    'status' => 'comfortable'
  );
}
```

How it works...

The two control structures explained here have much in common. In a single term, they can be termed as entry-controlled structures because they follow the **first-decide-then-do** principle. They were not designed to make you lament your actions (pun intended). There is a gunslinger control structure that lives by the gun and dies by it, the `do-while` loop. It can cause you to lament your decision if you do not pay proper attention while using it. In the same terminology, it is an exit-controlled structure and will execute the task at least once. While this can seem required in some scenarios, you are advised to refrain from using `do-while`. Take a look at the following screenshot:

```php
$pizzaDish = new PizzaDish('New Pizza', 'Dish');
$ingredients = array('salt','cheese','capsicum'
);

$ingredientCount = 0;
do {
  $pizzaDish->add($ingredients[$ingredientCount]);
  $ingredientCount++;
} while ($ingredientCount < count($ingredients));
```

So, in essence, the statement `$pizzaDish->add($ingredients[$ingredientCount])` gets executed at least once, increments the value of `$ingredientCount` by one, and then checks if the value is within limit. To use `do-while`, you need to place the cursor on the target statement and select the `do-while` option that appears in the **Select** dialog on going to **Code | Surround with**.

To make your application program responsible enough, you need to implement exception handling denoted by a **try-catch** block. A simple use case to demonstrate the usage of exception handling will be shown in this recipe. You are attempting to prepare your `PizzaDish`. You plan to put salt and cheese as usual and capsicum as toppings to make it WOW. While cooking, you discovered that there was no capsicum in the fridge! But you are hungry enough not to let anything come between you and your `PizzaDish`. You will add tomato in that case. So, where is the responsibility in this code? It is that during preparation in your code to handle an *exceptional* situation there was a topping missing, but the code took the responsibility and handled this exceptional situation by adding tomato in place of capsicum.

Your `PizzaDish` continued to cook in the following way:

```
$pizzaDish = new PizzaDish('New Pizza', 'Dish');
$ingredients = array( 'salt', 'cheese', '' );
$ingredientCount = 0;
try {
   while ($ingredientCount < count($ingredients)) {
      if ($ingredients[$ingredientCount] == '') {
         throw new Exception("\nYou have run out of capsicum.");
      } else {
         $pizzaDish->add($ingredients[$ingredientCount]);
         echo "\nWaiting for capsicum topping...";
      }
      $ingredientCount++;
   }
} catch (Exception $e) {
   echo $e->getMessage();
   $pizzaDish->add('tomato');
}
```

The following screenshot shows you how the which-control-to-surround looks. And it is worth noting that you should know which control structure you are going to use.

Finding the matching brace

If you embrace the brace, you will never be embarrassed.

Some PhpStorm Cookbook writer

Getting ready

Braces are an important element in programming. They not only define the boundary for the programmer, but also the interpreter. Both of you get to know the construct or from where to where the variable ranges. The PHP interpreter just needs to have a closing brace for every opening brace to proceed irrespective of how the code has been written. But the PHP interpreter is not powerful enough to write code for you—you have to do it yourself.

How to do it...

If you are provided with a small piece of code that is less than 100 lines long, you can somehow manage to read and maintain the code. If the line numbers exceed 100, code formatting comes to your rescue.

PhpStorm enables you to format all or some of the selected lines by simple mouse clicks or a single keyboard shortcut. To format code, you need to select **Code | Reformat Code**, and your code will be formatted like a charm.

The keyboard shortcut for this is *Ctrl + Alt + L*.

How it works...

After PhpStorm has formatted the code, life becomes easier for you. You can very easily find the matching brace by putting the cursor on the brace. The paired braces get highlighted automatically. This highlighting feature can be customized as well. You need to go to **File | Settings | Editor | Highlight on caret movement** and check or uncheck the **Highlight matched brace** checkbox to turn highlighting matching braces on or off. You can change the brace color, the background color of the brace, and so on. You can make your braces look bold or italic. In order to customize this behavior, you need to set up a new scheme. To start off, you need to go to **File | Settings | Editor | Colors & Fonts | Language Defaults | Brackets**, select one of the default themes, and do a **Save As** in order to make a copy, as shown in the following screenshot:

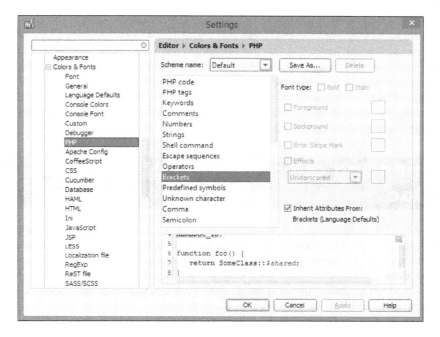

 The color scheme you just saved was saved as an XML document with the extension `.icls` under the `~/.WebIdeXX/config/colors` directory. The name of this document is the same as the name you provided while copying the color scheme.

There's more...

Let us now look at how to format a long string.

Wrapping string

Another important aspect of code formatting gains importance when you have written some really long strings or some really long statements. You might end up in trouble trying to read those long lines. Even if you managed to read it, you might end up being confused about the start and end of those long, unhandleable lines.

PhpStorm enables you to wrap long lines and statements according to a fixed width. You can ask PhpStorm to remember some limits for you by visiting the **File** | **Settings** | **Editor** | **Virtual Space** pane.

You can wrap the long lines in the editor by selecting the checkbox against the **Use Soft wraps in editor** option. Long lines don't torment you only in the editor. They can also create a usage torture sometimes when you use the PhpStorm terminal to execute command-line PHP. If you check the **Use Soft wraps in console** option, you can avoid this problem once and for all. PhpStorm makes a provision for you to set the indent level for the wrap in the console. If you select this checkbox, the wrapped long line will continue into the next line, but with the specified number of spaces. Now, you cannot complain that you are not sure which one is your wrapped line and which one is your original line!

Commenting out a section of code and PHPDoc

PHPDoc is a facility provided by PHP, which is meant to document the complex code that you toiled very hard to build. The importance of documenting code and properly documented code need not be explained to those of you who have taken care of someone else's code at some point in their lives. For all others, and for those who know, yet are hungry for knowledge, here are a few points that might explain why you should always document your code—no matter what and how. Stay tuned for some interesting use cases.

Getting ready

You planned to cook `PizzaDish`. How did you proceed? You created an entity called `Dish`, designed some functions in it that will assist you in adding some ingredients, and created a special case of the general case `Dish`. You named this particular case `PizzaDish`. In order to cook your pizza, you invoked `PizzaDish` and enjoyed eating your favorite pizza. Things went smoothly. But how many times does it happen that you do not cook other things? Can you spend your life just eating pizza? Don't you think that you have other tasks to perform? Here's the analogy. How many times does it happen that you need nothing other than your written code? Can you be a good programmer by just using your own class or code? Will you create algorithms for each and every task that you perform?

In short, do you believe in reinventing the wheel?

Normal people would answer no. For them, how do you use classes written by another fellow programmer? How did you discover that the function `Engine::start('car')` will turn the ignition on? This is where documentation comes in. It is the medium by which you were able to discover that a start method in the `Engine` class was meant to turn on the engine ignition.

Writing clean code is the first key to documentation. You should always think of names that explain a lot. You should always think of descriptive names. If you think you are running out of names, you can make use of PHP namespaces.

To start thinking about how to write clean code, you are requested to read this book thoroughly. To start writing clean code, you are requested to start writing code.

How to do it...

If you were careful enough and have a sharp memory, you would have already read the `Dish` and the `PizzaDish` classes. Looking at the way the variables were defined and the methods were declared, did you feel the need for other documentation? They say it and they say it right: *Good code in itself is good documentation*. But if you are unable to think of descriptive names in your code, here comes your savior—PHPDoc.

You have three ways to add comments to your code:

▸ Single line

▸ Multiline or block comment

▸ Documentation comment

In order to learn, you have to perform .In order to perform, you have to start. So let's start. Add comments to the `PizzaDish` class itself for clarity.

A single-line comment is the simplest and the easiest form of writing comments in PHP code. A single-line comment begins with `//`, and whatever follows in a single line is treated by the PHP engine as a single-line comment. In the `PizzaDish` class, a single-line comment has been added next to the list (php array) of ingredients, which looks like the following line of code:

```
// This is the list of ingredients that you plan to add
```

In order to write a single-line comment in PhpStorm, you need to take care of the location of the comment.

 You can write the comment without the need to begin it with `//`. When you are done with your sentence, you can use the shortcut *Ctrl + /*, and PhpStorm will happily convert the statement to a single-line comment.

Can your life be restricted to write a single line of comment? What if you want to have a number of single-line comments? Multiline or block comments will be required.

All you need to do is to identify the precious code extent, and add `/*` at the beginning and `*/` at the end of the code. There are people in this world who do not have an idea of what *precious* is. All good software engineers will ignore such people and move on. In the `PizzaDish` class discussed, you can see that the last few lines were commented out. This is a block comment. In the current scenario, your taste buds were the business end, people!

Documentation comments start with /** and end with */. Does it not look like the block comment? A more careful examination would tell you the difference.

While a block comment just needs a comment starting symbol and an ending symbol, a documentation comment requires a * symbol before the start of every line. While the PHP engine skips the contents inside the block (and the single-line) comments, the PHP engine (actually, the documentation engine) "peeps" into the documentation lines when generating the actual beautiful comments. Where do you get to see the documents? Dear, when you press *Ctrl + Q* over any method declaration, what do you see? Yes, it is a document that is the same as generated by the documentation engine. Magic? PhpStorm's magic.

Fireworks! Too long? Didn't read? A step-by-step explanation follows:

```
/**
 * Class PizzaDish
 *
 * Bake a new type of <strong>Dish</strong>.
 * This dish has the following features:
 * <ul>
 * <li>It eases the appetite</li>
 * <li>It makes the taste buds happy</li>
 * <li>It confirms to the software engineering practises</li>
 * <li>It teaches engineers various aspects of PHP
programming</li>
 * </ul>
 */
```

How it works...

This is probably the first documentation comment you are looking into. You will be surprised to know that the HTML tags you write here are actually processed by the PHP documentation engine. The output of the documentation comment appears when you put the cursor over the target member and go to **View | Quick Documentation**:

A picture is worth a thousand words. You can easily see how the HTML tags were processed to give proper formatting to the document.

Similarly, you can add documentation to your methods as well (the same class and the same method, but this time, it's setDishName with added documentation). The documentation lines would be as follows:

```
/**
 * <strong>Setter</strong> method for giving a name to your
Pizza<br/><br/>
 * In order to set values for the members variables, it is
<em>advised</em> to use setter methods.
 * @param string $dishName The name of the dish you want to
create.
 */
```

You just used the HTML strong tag to emphasize the type of the method setDishName. You were also able to emphasize that software engineering principles advise the use of setter methods. The comment for this method takes the following form:

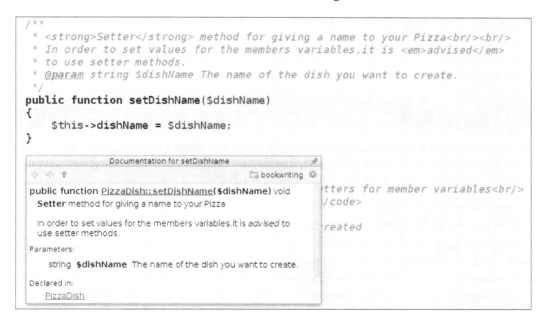

In order to use the keyboard shortcut *Ctrl + Q*, you need not necessarily place your cursor under the method name. This works for the documentation comment region as well. PhpStorm is smart, so it understands that and shows you the same documentation.

PhpStorm never disappoints you. There is a facility in PhpStorm in which you can customize the way your documentation comment should look. To do that, you need to go to **File | Settings | Code Style | PHP | PHPDoc**, as shown in the following screenshot. The options are quite descriptive.

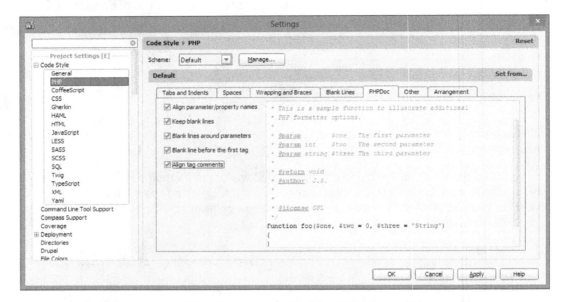

Creating a working set

You would have felt a number of times that different PHP projects have different priorities. You got it right. A website development project, for example, would require a running web server configuration, and it might not require command-line PHP.

Getting ready

A simple PHP project, on the other hand, would require command-line PHP, without a web server, and the list of directories could be limited to some folders in a hierarchy. The point here is that there are different projects with different dependencies and settings. Having a working set makes PhpStorm behave appropriately for the project currently open.

How to do it...

If you monitor the **Settings** pane closely, you will notice that there are two major sections. One is the project-settings section, where you make settings according to your project. This helps a great deal. PhpStorm builds an index for every project. If you create a proper working set for your project, you will help PhpStorm to build a more precise index, and the project processing will be much faster. Some of the important settings are:

- ▶ **PHP Specific Settings**: Making settings to execute the application you plan to create is quite handy. You need not to worry about how to execute and test your application. You just need to choose from a list of options that PhpStorm will put up before you.

- ▶ **Interpreter**: You could be required to implement some offline tasks on your web hosting service, which could probably do an update, a check, log cleaning tasks, and so on. You might configure command-line PHP for such files so that you can access them by a direct keyboard shortcut.

- ▶ **Webserver**: Most of the time, you need to have a web server to run your PHP web application code. For this, you can specify the settings for the web server in PhpStorm.

- ▶ **Debugger**: Life without a debugger for a web developer is like life for a doctor without a stethoscope. When you don't know what is going on inside, how can you find out what is actually going on? You require a debugger for sure.

- ▶ **Directories**: PhpStorm builds indexes of the files and folders that are there in the project. A longer index list means more memory consumption. Exclude unwanted *directory(ies)* from indexing, and PhpStorm will be grateful to you.

- ▶ **Inspections**: PhpStorm acts as an inspector for the code you write. By default, there are a number of inspections that are on, and in most probability, you would not require all of them at all times.

- ▶ **Version Control**: If you are working in a team, having a versioning system is the need of the hour. You can set the details of the versioning system, such as the URL, the username, the password, and all the necessary details that will make your life easier when downloading (checking out) or uploading (committing) in the project that a team is working on.

The other one is the IDE-specific settings section. This provides you with control over the configurations that are universally true for all projects under PhpStorm. The description is beyond the scope of this topic.

Creating TODO tasks

Suppose it is the end of day, you have to *hurry home* (no pun intended), there are fantastic ideas overflowing in your mind, and you are quite sure that you will not be able to regenerate those ideas. You can ask TODO to come to your assistance in those cases.

Getting ready

A **TODO** tag, when added to some PHP code, makes it visible under the TODO view. You can also refer to the TODO section of this chapter for a refresher.

Considering the same Dish and the PizzaDish scenario, suppose you thought of having some system to check whether the dish is cooked, you can put a flag there and then. This flag will keep reminding you about this.

How to do it...

To do a TODO, all you need to do is write TODO, followed by the reminder text, and press *Ctrl + /* (that is comment the code). From what you have learned already, you can now document your Dish class. Probably, it would look something like the following code snippet:

```
class Dish {
  /**
   * Add some ingredients to your dish. <br/>
   * You can do that by specifying the name of the ingredient.
   *
   * @param string $ingredientName The name of the ingredient to be
added
   */
  public function add($ingredient){
    echo "\nYou have added: ", $ingredient;
  }

//    TODO Add some method to check if the pizza is cooked
}
```

You managed to keep the functionality intact; you just added documentation comments for the class and the member methods. Everything else is as usual; the only alien item is the TODO. So, as you can see, a simple TODO was added. People might argue the usage of TODO. They are right and wrong in saying that life can be managed without TODO. They are right only in the case of tiny projects, where there is not much code and simple comments are visible and easily remembered. They are absolutely wrong in all other (and real-world) cases, where there are uncountable lines of code and you could actually face a nightmare in trying to figure out where you placed a comment related to some suggestion. PhpStorm is able to extract all the TODOs from your project and show them accurately in the TODO view.

How it works...

Besides reminding you of some tasks-be-done-in-future, there can be some **FIXME** tags as well. As the name suggests, FIXME tags can be used to denote some feature that has produced errors or is prone to producing errors. You just need to use the FIXME keyword, followed by the description, which is then followed using *Ctrl + /* (commenting). PhpStorm will start showing it in the TODO section, as shown in the following code:

```
public function add($ingredient){
   echo "\nYou have added: ", $ingredient;
   //  FIXME Check for a valid ingredient name
}
```

The fixme (or FIXME) tag will start indicating that there is something that has to be fixed.

However, the game's not over with TODO. If there are a number of fellow programmers in your development team, you can add flags for an individual teammate. How? PhpStorm provides you with filters. This is available at **File** | **Settings** | **TODO**.

You need to add a new pattern and a new filter to make it available in the filters section in the TODO view. On adding it, you will be able to set the flag for a particular fellow programmer. The code with this new flag looks like the following snippet:

```
public function add($ingredient){
   echo "\nYou have added: ", $ingredient;
   //  FIXME Check for a valid ingredient name
}


//  TODO Add some method to check if the pizza is cooked
//  TODO for ALice Please add the appropriate usecase for the
checking functionality
```

The filters and the patterns are case-insensitive by default because a programmer's life already has a number of issues to handle. Keep this in mind!

Will you able to do the TODO?

```php
    public function add($ingredient){
        echo "\nYou have added: ", $ingredient;
//        FIXME Check for a valid ingredient name
    }

//    TODO Add some method to check if the pizza is cooked
//    TODO for ALice Please add the appropriate usecase for the checking functionality
}
```

TODO: Project   ▾

▼ Found 3 TODO items in 1 file
  ▼ 📄 Dish.php
    📄 (28, 11) //   FIXME Check for a valid ingredient name
    📄 (31, 7) // TODO Add some method to check if the pizza is cooked
    📄 (32, 7) // TODO for ALice Please add the appropriate usecase for the checking functionality

3
Refactoring and Building

In this chapter, we will cover the following recipes:

- ▶ Renaming elements
- ▶ Copying elements
- ▶ Moving elements
- ▶ Moving a method
- ▶ Moving a variable
- ▶ Deleting elements
- ▶ Searching code in a project
- ▶ Comparing files
- ▶ Restoring elements using comparison
- ▶ Setting the run configuration
- ▶ Running your code

Introduction

Grandma's advice: stick to software engineering.

Software engineering advice: emphasize on code reusability. Any code base engineered according to the software engineering paradigm will be reusable. That is to say, you can use your code forever having written it once. They say "Write once, use forever".

Revisiting the pizza baking use case, you will observe that in order to cook whatever dish, you just had to use the `add` function since you stuck to the mentioned paradigm. Suppose there are 50 different types of dishes that you are about to cook. Each dish is different in itself, but each will require the `add` method. If you convert this into technology, you will, in most cases, inherit the `Dish` class. That is your `PizzaDish`. The methods of the `Dish` class are reused in all the classes such as `PizzaDish`.

If you want to change the business logic, you can happily and comfortably change the logic inside the method body, and the changes will be reflected in all of the classes that inherit (or use) this class.

So far, so good...but if you were to change the signature of the method inside the base class itself, what will you do? Yes, this can arise in the initial phase of development when the plans change a bit and thus lead to change in the use case.

Renaming elements

As the saying goes, change is inevitable; you must be ready for change, whatever the timeline might be. Engineers are negligent enough to commit mistakes while renaming—typographical errors, forgetting where to change, and so on. Don't worry, you can at least rest assured with PhpStorm at your disposal. What PhpStorm does is that it provides a refactoring system, in which you can make your change penetrate throughout the project, visible in one single step: **The Refactoring Step**. If you opt for refactoring, you have the freedom to do a number of refactoring tasks.

So, an `addIngredient` method can be easily written as `addingredient` at some point in code; `toolTip` can be written as `tootLip`, and so on. There might be five places in your code where you used the method `addSalt`, but when you changed the method signature of `add`, somehow you forgot and changed it in only four locations in your code base. Such petty mistakes can be safely termed as silly mistakes but might cause more damage than you can imagine. They eat up the most valuable resource—time. You will end up realizing that it was just a typographical error or a slip but only to realize that you crossed over the deadline.

With refactoring, you can safely rename a method signature and tell PhpStorm to penetrate this change by finding and making the same change across all the occurrences.

Refactoring applies to all the elements of code: class names, method names, method signatures, variable names, and so on. PhpStorm treats them alike! Justice PhpStorm!

A directory in a PHP project is much like the package in Java—if you ever had a previous encounter with the Java programming language. In simple words, a directory in a PHP project is a grouping for classes. You can group similar classes in directories. Thus, your controller classes might be under your controller directory, model classes under model directory, configuration files under the `config` directory, and so on. Directories are important. Consider this, if you wish to change the name of a particular directory, you need to refactor it. You need to rename it. Thus, all those lines of code that refer to a class (`include, include once` or `require, require_once`) will be automatically updated once you rename a particular directory.

How to do it...

The elements that we are going to rename are directories and classes; let's have a look at them one by one.

Renaming a directory

To rename a directory, perform the following steps:

1. In order to rename a directory, you need to access the right-click on the context menu and select the **Rename** option.

2. On providing the new name, you can choose whether to let this change penetrate throughout the project wherever this directory has been referenced.

3. You can also choose whether you want to replace the occurrence in comments and strings as well. This is shown in the following screenshot:

 If you wish to see which occurrences are there corresponding to this directory, you can select the **Preview** button, or else, you can directly **Refactor** the changes. Once you have refactored the changes, you can sit back and concentrate on further development plans.

Renaming a class

Sometimes, even the best plan cannot be guaranteed to be foolproof. You might have started to go east, but due to the wind current, you felt that going southeast was a better and feasible option. Plan destroyed? Not at all—some amendments are required, and then you are good to go.

Here's a use case—you planned to cook some `Dish` and went to the kitchen, but you found out that the essential ingredients were missing. What will you do? Remain hungry? Not at all... You will proceed to cook some other dish that is a `Dish`. In order to proceed, you will try to reuse some of the logic that you used in `PizzaDish`. In technical terms, you will need to rename (refactor) your class.

How it works...

In order to do that (refactor your class), you need to place your cursor over the class name, access the right-click context menu, and select **Rename**. You can do **Preview** to check for which occurrences will be changed, and once you are convinced, you can do **Refactor**.

Simple, isn't it? Indeed.

The refactoring in this case will look as shown in the following screenshot:

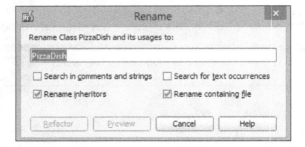

There's more...

Until now, we were familiar with renaming elements. Now, it is time to see how a method can be renamed.

Renaming a method

Refactoring in the case of methods in PhpStorm provides you with a fine-grained control to make changes in either the name of the method or the method signature. To change the method name is easy. Similar to renaming a directory and renaming a class, you need to place your cursor over the target method name, access the right-click context menu and proceed to **Rename**. You can apply the changes in the box specified. If you want to preview, you can **Preview**, or else you can **Refactor**, and PhpStorm will happily propagate the changes across the occurrences.

Renaming member variables

Of all the renaming criteria and explanations provided, renaming a member variable is the most typical, and it requires the most amount of maturity in handling. In short, this one is a "handle with care" situation. Variables can be local or global or scope-based. You require a variable name, $salt, for the ingredient salt to be added to PizzaDish and another $salt for algorithmic purposes—say to add random characters to your password to make the container for the cooked dish more safe. Thus, you want some salt to cook your dish as well as to prevent others from eating it.

In order to rename a variable carefully, the steps are the same as those described in the previous cases—the addition is the warning *CAREFUL*. You need to place your cursor over the variable name, access the right-click on the context menu, and select **Rename**, and PhpStorm will display all of the occurrences. You can select from the available list and selectively rename the required occurrences.

See also...

You can also refer to the renaming method and renaming directory in previous sections.

Changing the method signature is not difficult either. In plural cases, you might realize that passing an extra argument will do the trick for you. So, you have the magic wand PhpStorm with which you can very easily do the magic to make this happen.

You can start by placing the cursor over the method name, accessing the right-click context menu, and selecting **Change the Method Signature**. The magic begins.

PhpStorm provides you with many options to change the signature of the target method. You can refer to the previous chapter, where changing the method signature has been described in detail.

To avoid the need to change a method signature just for the sake of adding or deleting parameters, you can use PHP func_get_args(), by which you can make your method independent from the hassles of parameters. Thus, you just need to create a method with no parameters and use func_get_args() to get all the arguments, 1, 5, or even 35 easily. You might ask "why in the world would we use parameters then?" The answer to this is rather short. You should have mercy on the PHP interpreter; it has to do more processing in that case.

Copying elements

A directory contains classes, classes contain methods and variables, methods contain variables, and methods use variables.

The point to prove is that everything is related in one way or another. You can equally want to copy a directory, as you want to copy a class safely to some location other than the current location or declaration.

How to do it...

Copying a directory means that somewhere, some concept has changed, which led to a regrouping of the classes. So, it will be better to think again. If you are still determined, you need to perform the following step:

 ▶ Go to **Project View**, (*Alt + 1*), highlight the target directory, access the right-click context menu, go to **Refactor**, and then choose the **Copy** option. PhpStorm will ask you for the details. The details will be the new name, and the target directory under which you wish to copy the directory to. PhpStorm will copy that for you.

There is one more way to achieve the same effect for a directory:

 ▶ You can also directly copy a directory from one location to another by the same old *Ctrl + C* and *Ctrl + V* combination.

For a directory, it creates the same effect the difference lies in the way they work. Refactor is a more PhpStorm way to copy; it does not save anything to the clipboard.

How it works...

Copying is more an operating system approach. It copies the name as a string value in the clipboard. So, you can paste the name as-is inside the editor and paste the directory as-is in the project view. Interesting, isn't it?

The copy directory looks as it does in the following screenshot:

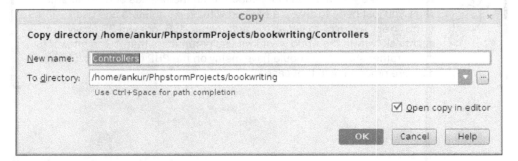

Which one should you choose then? It's your call. Do either, but make sure you follow the **Don't Repeat Yourself** (**DRY**) principle.

As of now, you are familiar with copying the elements, and now it is time to move to copying a class.

Copying a class

Copying a class means copying the business logic in most scenarios. In software engineering, a sophisticated name given to this process is **Off-The-Shelf** development. You can cheat everyone but not yourself, you copycat! A class is copied in order to reuse most of the existing business logic that exists in it. More logic is, however, pumped into the class to inflate it. To copy a class and start your Off-The-Shelf development, you need to copy a class by accessing the right-click context menu and selecting the **Copy** option. The dialog box is similar. The questions are similar. The effect is similar. The outcome is different. Here, a single class is copied from one location to another.

Like you can do a copy-paste for a directory, you could do exactly the same for a class of your choice. Following the operating system way of copying, the name of the class to be copied is placed on the clipboard as well. If you paste it in an editor, the name of the class will be pasted, and if you paste the name of the class in the Project view, the class as a whole will be pasted inside the Project view at the selected location.

Moving elements

Any keen software engineer knows the importance of cut or copy and paste. The information associated with this important statement is given here:

► Cutting and pasting is faster than copying and pasting. However, cutting and pasting changes the location of the selected element. Also, copying keeps the original in place, whereas cutting removes it from where it was.

Any dedicated software engineer will already have this knowledge through past experience.

How to do it...

We have talked about renaming elements, copying elements, and now, it's time to move a directory.

Moving a directory

If you are sure that somewhere, your architecture has changed in such a way that your grouping has changed, you should be prepared to move an entire directory (your grouping) to some other grouping (some other directory or location). In order to move a directory, you need to perform the following steps:

1. You need to go to the Project view, select the desired directory (also known as grouping), access the right-click context menu, and select the **Move** option.

2. PhpStorm will ask you a single question as to where you want to move this selected directory.

3. Once you answer, PhpStorm will take care of the rest of the things, and your task will be accomplished.

Moving a class

You want to move your class to some other directory (or namespace, folder, or grouping in the most layman terminology) ideally in some case where you started off your development in haste without a proper plan and now you realize that what you thought your entity will be like was not the best solution possible. OK, don't blame yourself. Instead, use PhpStorm to help you refactor your class by moving it to a more appropriate place. The command to do this is the same.

Use the right-click context menu, refactor, and move. Specify the location of the target directory where you want to relocate this class to. PhpStorm will prompt you on completion.

Moving a method

There are two prerequisites to moving a method to some other class. One is the most common prerequisite: you should be clear about what you are doing. The other is that the method to be moved must be static. If it is not, PhpStorm will alert you by saying **Move non-static method is not supported**.

How to do it...

To move the method, perform the following steps:

1. Just place the cursor over the method name, and access the **Refactor** option from the right-click context menu and move.

2. You need to provide the name of the target class where you wish to move this method.

3. You have the option to preview which occurrences will be affected by this change (movement).

4. Once you are happy with the proposed results, you can refactor the method. The target class will now contain the method you just moved, as shown in the following screenshot:

Moving a variable

Moving a member variable to some other class is simple but quite important from an architectural point of view. A variable usually denotes an attribute from the real world. So, if you planned sugar for `PizzaDish`, you will definitely and very quickly need to move the sugar from `PizzaDish` to some other dish, say `Cookie`. Just like methods, you can only move the static members to some other class.

How to do it...

Select **Refactor** from the right-click context menu, and then select **Move**.

If the current member variable to be moved was private in the current class, the **Move** operation will convert the member to public.

PhpStorm warns you before performing the move, as shown in the following screenshot:

 Wherever you put the sugar, you should always try to use the syntactic sugar because it eases a bit of the documentation load.

PhpStorm said "Your knowledge level has been increased to 200 percent". You must say "Great!"... 200 percent... how? You already knew how to copy or cut and paste under the operating system you were comfortable with. 100 percent knowledge... Now you know a PhpStorm way to do the same plus 100 percent knowledge. So, applying simple mathematics, your knowledge level is now 200 percent"

Besides this refactoring by moving, you can also play around with your code by moving any program construct or identifier across the code. This is not refactoring but simple moving. PhpStorm can be configured to respect your `if-else` or other blocks of code. To move a line of code, you just need to place your cursor over the desired line and use the magical shortcut *Alt + Shift + Up* or *Down*. Your line will be moved up or down. This action works well for a selection of code as well.

Deleting elements

The deletion of code from the code base is itself a very daring task. Asking a programmer to delete business logic in the code is like asking for one of the kidneys!

Getting ready

PhpStorm attempts to ease this by providing a **Safe Delete** option. You can delete an element in your code by refactoring it. This refactoring will find the occurrences of the selected element, and as soon as you ask it to proceed, PhpStorm happily deletes the selected occurrences of the element in your project.

How to do it...

To delete a file, you need to follow these steps:

1. Access the right-click context menu after placing the cursor over the target filename.

2. Choose the **Safe Delete** option. PhpStorm then asks you whether you want to look into the comments and strings inside your code, as shown in the following screenshot:

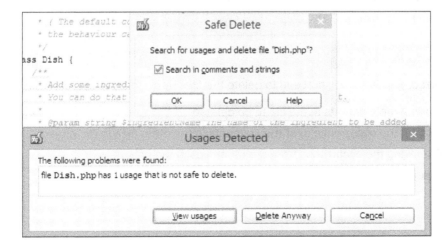

3. If you continue, PhpStorm will let you know of any potential problems in deleting the file.

4. You can then have a look at the list of files that are under the radar by selecting the **View usages** options or pressing *Alt + F7*.

5. PhpStorm will provide you with a list of the files that have references to what you are deleting. If you change your mind, you can rerun safe delete. If you are determined enough, you can proceed to delete. If you choose not to delete, you can cancel this process altogether, as shown in the following screenshot:

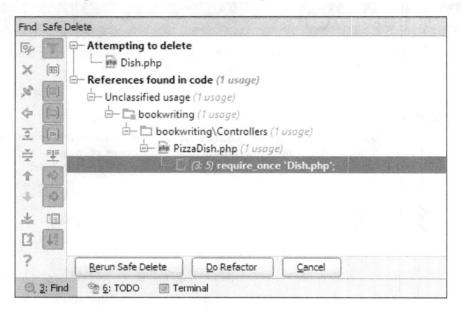

6. If you are happy with the consequences of the delete process, you can choose the **Delete Anyway** option.

How it works...

Once finalized, PhpStorm will proceed to delete the files by performing the following actions:

►   Finding the elements in the file to be deleted

►   Finding the occurrence(s) of the elements in the other files in the project

►   Removing the occurrence from the other files in the project

►   Deleting the file that was selected initially

Searching code in a project

It is highly unlikely that anyone will remember each and every line of code. If your manager scolds you for not having remembered the last line where you made a certain change, all you need to do is to smile and continue working with PhpStorm. When you forget while typing where you kept your wireless keyboard or when you can forget where you kept your car keys while driving the same car, you can forget anything. Humans can forget anything. The human brain acts in unexplained ways.

Getting ready

Having PhpStorm by your side means that you can afford to forget about your code. Even if you have some memory of keywords such as Pizza or Dish, there are facilities available in PhpStorm where you can find all mentions of these keywords. Are you still not convinced about the success of this power of PhpStorm? Stay tuned for more information.

Within PhpStorm, there is a **Find in path** tool. It is one of the best features provided by PhpStorm from the technical and usage perspectives. Technically, it is programmed to be smart while at the same time being fast. If you somehow happen to search something that PhpStorm thinks could become an issue, it warns you by showing you an alert, as shown in the following screenshot:

How to do it...

The journey to search for an item in the project begins with a simple and easy-to-remember keyboard shortcut, *Ctrl + Shift + F*. As soon as you initiate the command, you will be asked to provide your search parameters.

The first option you are provided is the string you want to search for. This is the most basic and the most important requirement needed for the search to proceed.

If you don't provide any text, the **Find** button cannot perform a search. The text that you enter here should be provided strategically to save your and PhpStorm's time. The following example with multiple perspectives is the best. Assume that you are very hungry and need to know how to cook pizza. Your search string will be `pizza`.

You can narrow down the search criteria, as shown in the following screenshot:

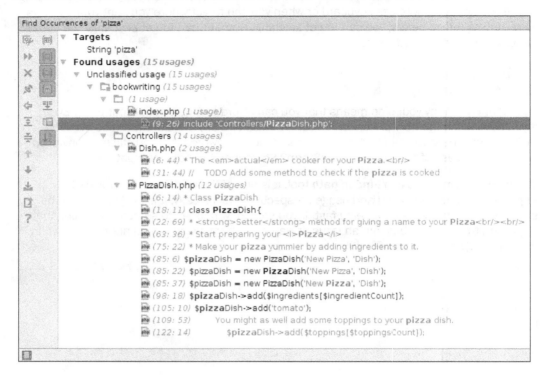

There is a **Directory** radio button in the pop up. You can select that in order to let PhpStorm know that it has to select inside a particular directory only. When you specify the path to the target directory, PhpStorm will perform the same task of searching, but this time it will do so with narrowed-down search criteria. The point worth noting here is that a project is just a collection of directories, so when you search in a project, you actually search in a set of directories and/or certain files. When you select a directory, you thus make the search faster because PhpStorm has to search less. Lazy PhpStorm!

If there are directories inside the target directory, you can tell PhpStorm to actually descend into the directories by selecting the **Recursively** option, as shown in the following screenshot:

However, you might still need to work through many results to find the target.

If you want to tell PhpStorm to search in certain files, you can do that by selecting one of the following values from the drop-down box next to the **Custom** scope:

- ▶ **Project Files**: The search will be limited to the project files.
- ▶ **Projects and Libraries**: The search will include the project directory and the libraries that are used in the project.
- ▶ **Project Test Files**: The search will look into the test files for the project.
- ▶ **Open Files**: The search will look into the files that are currently open in the editor.
- ▶ **Files in previous search results**: The search will look into the files that were used in the previous searches. This means PhpStorm remembers what you searched for.

If you want to have your own custom search criteria, you can do that as well. PhpStorm will record your preferences and allow you to switch to them whenever you want to search. To do that, there is the button next to the custom dropdown. When you press that, you will be asked to save your preferences, as shown in the following screenshot:

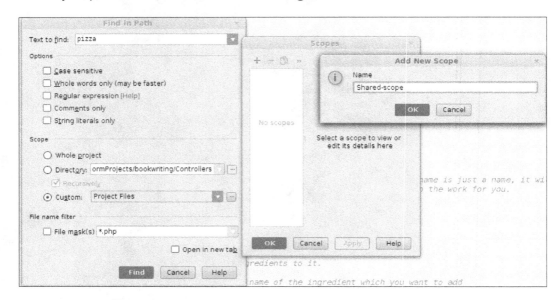

As soon as you hit the **Save** button, your preferences will start appearing in the same dropdown under the division, **Custom** scopes. If, at some point in the future, you need to change the custom search scope you just created, you need to follow the same steps. The same form will appear, and you can edit your preferences from there.

How it works...

You still have a lot to search. The human mind is very lazy, and it always looks for better alternatives that consume less energy. Searching inside the project was a bit too much. You still have to look into the search results manually and then decide which one your desired version of pizza is, as shown in the following screenshot:

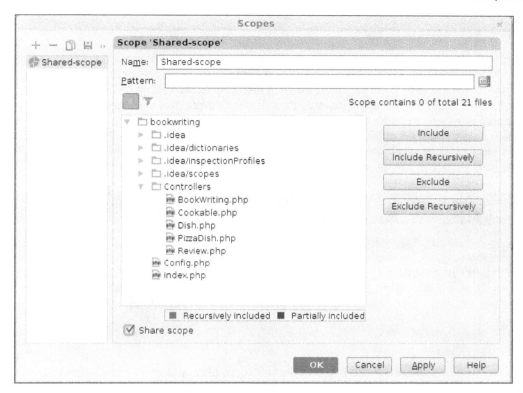

Your `pizza` could have been a `Pizza`. In that case, you need to select the **Case Sensitive** option. PhpStorm will differentiate between `Pizza` and `pizza`.

If you are sure that you just want to search for a pizza, you should check the **Whole words only** option. Thus, PhpStorm will know that it has to search pizza only and not the likes of `pizzadish`, `pizzacooking`, or `pizzacooked`.

If you just want to search for the occurrence of `pizza` inside comments (PHPDoc included), you need to select the **Comments only** option.

If you just want to find out how many strings contain the word `pizza`, you should select the **String literals only** option. PhpStorm will look at the string constants only.

There's more...

The most important part of searching appears when you decide that you are going to search for all those cases in which there is `pizza` at the end or in the middle or at the beginning. By now, regular expressions may start to ring a bell. Your search string can probably be like `^pizza` if you are interested in all words that start with pizza. You then need to select the **Regular expression** option. You will obviously want to create more and more use cases in order to master the art of **RegEx**. For help with regard to the usage of RegEx, you can head to the help section in PhpStorm. For ease, the same table has been copied here. People familiar with Java will feel at home!

Comparing files

Changed code is a nightmare. This is unanimously agreed by the community of developers across the world. To control change, there are versioning systems available. These can show you in detail that a file has changed whenever you upload your changed file to the versioning server. However, who is responsible for the changes you make to your local working copy? How are you going to track which change caused your code to break down?

Getting ready

You can use file comparisons. Since PhpStorm records each and every activity that you perform on the editor, you can find out the actual nonworking code by comparing your troublesome file across different timelines. If you feel *timelines* is an alien here, you might feel easy to know that PhpStorm actually saves your local copy versions according to timestamps. If at some point in time, your code stops working and undo will not help, you can use file comparison to review the timeline and compare the historical file with your current file. You will then be able to identify which change was the culprit in preventing your code from executing.

How to do it...

In order to view the local history and compare the current file with the historical file, perform the following steps:

1. You need to access the right-click context menu, select the **local history** option, and select the **Show history** option.

2. You will be given details of the differences according to the timestamp of the file's history, as shown in the following screenshot:

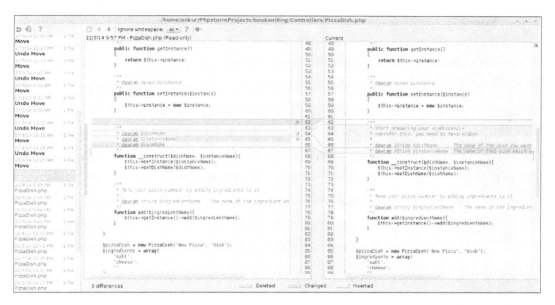

3. Similarly, you can compare two files with each other. You need to go to the project view, select the two files of interest, access the right-click context menu, and select the **Compare 2 files** option. You will be presented with a similar comparison window that shows any differences between the two files you selected.

4. The blue lines show changed content, the green line shows new content, and the red line shows conflicted content.

5.　There are directional arrows(**>>** and **<<**), which indicate which change should be passed on to which file, as shown in the following screenshot:

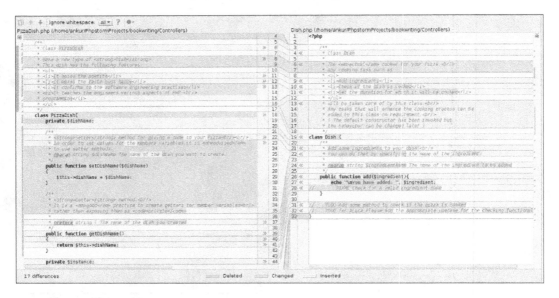

How it works...

If you don't like the colors, you can change them as well by navigating to **File** | **Settings** | **Editor** | **Colors & Fonts** | **Diff** in your destination, as shown in the following screenshot:

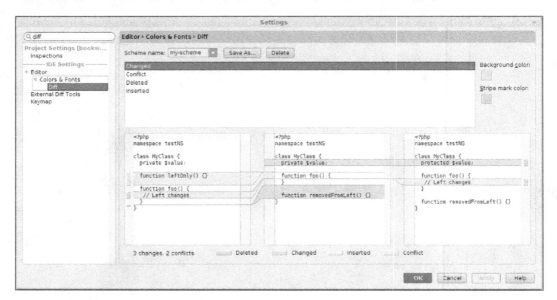

Sometimes, you have to live with someone else's noncompliance with software engineering practices. Such cases appear when you work in a team. A team member has, by mistake, made some changes to the code and pushed it to the code base. Being the senior programmer, you are asked to swing into action and fix that. But you don't have a clue as to how to proceed. You can use the same difference (or file comparison system) to compare the files in the repository itself. Once you compare it with the last few revisions, you will, in no time at all, discover the error and will be able to fix it. Thus, you will prove your worth as a programmer! Thanks PhpStorm.

Whatever comparison you do and whichever files you compare, the keyboard shortcut is *Ctrl + D* by default. It is expected that you will remember this. Remembering this shortcut is applicable to compare only when the change history window is open.

Restoring elements using comparison

Besides file comparison, this difference system can be a great deal of help if you wish to recover deleted files or folders. You just need to remember the name of the directory in which the deleted file was initially located. Will that relate to the problem? Yes, it will. If you view the local history of the folder, you will be able to see which actions have been performed on the directory.

Getting ready

The actions could be anything: new files or folders, a change in some of the files or folders, deletion of files or folders, and so on. You can now safely thank PhpStorm for monitoring each and every action you perform.

Once you find out the resource you were missing the most, you can revert to a timestamp that was just prior to the disastrous change.

How to do it...

The simplest way to restore changes is to use the keyboard shortcut *Ctrl + Z* to undo. You will be able to undo your previous edit in the file until you close it. The same is true for projects as well.

You can undo deletions, renames, or any changes that your project has. These are safe and PhpStorm keeps a record of all the history.

How it works...

Restoring the file is based on timestamps, or it can be restored using SVN or other versioning tools. We have discussed that undo is useful in software engineering, but the working of that is based on your operating system, which is beyond the scope of this book.

See also

This recovery process is already described in *Restoring Deleted Resources*.

 The only prerequisite is that the deletion process should be carried out inside PhpStorm only. If the resource was deleted outside it, PhpStorm will not be able to help.

Setting the run configuration

Having learned how to code within the PhpStorm editing system, you should be able to execute your code now. No, no! It is not being assumed that you don't know how to run code—the perspective being discussed here is PhpStorm. You can now read the mentioned statement again.

How to do it...

1. Run configuration can be set for the project-wide files. To make the configurations, you need to go to **Run | Edit Configurations** from the main menu. A dialog will appear that asks you a number of questions. The answers will assist you by providing a quicker way to execute your code.

2. Once you open the settings area, you need to broadly concentrate on the methods that are of interest to you. If you do not specify any settings, PhpStorm will determine the type of the scripts that you have written. The PHP script settings are an emulation of the scenario when you used to execute a PHP script via the command line by providing command-line arguments, specifying interpreter options or environment variables in case you wished to do something wild.

The arguments you specify are the command-line arguments to your PHP script.

The interpreter options are the options that you used to provide to your PHP interpreter. Some commonly used switches will make you recall those painful days: -a, -v, --info, and so on.

The following is a list of options available:

Options	Description
-a	Run as interactive shell.
-c<path>|<file>	Look for `php.ini` file in this directory.
-n	No `php.ini` file will be used.
-d foo[=bar]	Define INI entry `foo` with value `bar`.
-e	Generate extended information for debugger/profiler.
-f<file>	Parse and execute `<file>`.
-h	This is help.
-i	This gives PHP information.
-l	Syntax check only (lint).
-m	Show code compiled in modules.
-r<code>	Run PHP `<code>` without using script tags `<?...?>`.
-B<begin_code>	Run PHP `<begin_code>` before processing input lines.
-R<code>	Run PHP `<code>` for every input line.
-F<file>	Parse and execute `<file>` for every input line.
-E<end_code>	Run PHP `<end_code>` after processing all input lines.
-H	Hide any passed arguments from external tools.
-S<addr>:<port>	Run with built-in web server.
-t<docroot>	Specify document root `<docroot>` for built-in web server.
-s	Output HTML syntax highlighted source.
-v	This gives the version number.
-w	Output source with stripped comments and whitespace.
-z<file>	Load Zend extension `<file>`.
args...	Arguments passed to script. Use `--args` when first argument starts with - or the script is read from `stdin`.
--ini	Show configuration file names.
--rf<name>	Show information about function `<name>`.
--rc<name>	Show information about class `<name>`.
--re<name>	Show information about extension `<name>`.
--rz<name>	Show information about Zend extension `<name>`.
--ri<name>	Show configuration for extension `<name>`.

On saving the settings, your PHP script will be ready to be run.

It is worth noting here that this is just a PhpStorm way of executing the command-line PHP scripts. If you remember that there is a terminal view available in PhpStorm, you will easily relate that you can do the same tasks in the terminal as well.

The other configuration worth your interest is the PHP Web Application settings. It appears to lay people or nonprogrammers that web programming is an easy cake.

Happy are those who reject the advice of evil men and who do not follow the example of sinners.

How it works...

Thinking that web programming is easy, is like thinking that everyone can bake tasty pizza. Bear in mind that tasty is the word. To handle the challenge of executing a web-based application, you need to tell PhpStorm some facts that are basically settings. The settings you need to specify here are:

> A valid web server needs to be specified where your application will be launched. To configure a new server, there is a small square button to the right-hand side of the dropdown provided. Clicking on that, you are taken to an all-new settings area where you need to set up a web server.
>
> Complications! Go find those who say web programming is easy. You are free to do what you want with them, but here, with PhpStorm, you need to specify the configurations to set up a web server. To set up a new web server, you need to specify the name that you will use to address this web server in the future (near or far). You need to set the hostname (you'll probably be using localhost or 127.0.0.1) and the port number (the most common case will lead you to keep 80 as the value here). You can also specify a debugger here.
>
> By default, PhpStorm supports **Xdebug** and **zend-debugger**. Don't scratch your head as to what a debugger is. It will be taken up later in this book. Some developers prefer keeping their web server document root clean by only putting symbolic links inside it. The symbolic links point to some other location on the local disk. The reason for this is that the document root might not provide sufficient permissions that are required to write into a directory. You can obviously control your own directory more easily than the server's document root. If you have some symbolic links inside the document root, you can tell PhpStorm about it too. The left-hand side of the table is the actual path under which your project is saved, and to the right-hand side is the symbolic link under your document root.
>
> You can specify the start URL (base URL in spoken language). This is simple.

▶ The browser in which you need to view the web application needs to be specified too. You can select the browser from a list of predefined browsers. If you think you need to be specifically targeting certain browsers to view your code in, you need to go to the **Web Browsers** settings. This can be reached via two ways:

❑ The square button onto the right-hand side of the browser dropdown. The options that you get to fill in are the browser-related configurations. You can tell PhpStorm to follow the operating system underlying the selected default browser. You can select from either Firefox, Internet Explorer, Safari, Chrome, or Opera by selecting the path where the executable lies. You can also set a web browser as active or inactive and make a browser the default. You can use the browser settings with PhpStorm.

❑ The other one is via **File | Settings | Web Browsers**. Both the paths take you to the same destination, which is as follows:

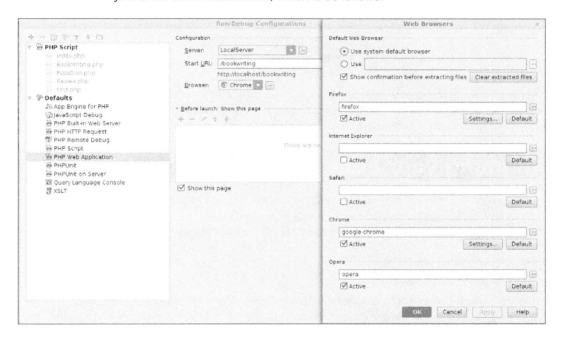

There are lots of web browsers available across the world. You can select a web browser of your choice and set it here for use in PhpStorm.

There's more...

You can also set a pre-run configuration by setting some command that is executed just before your application gets executed. There are certain options available for configuration. You can even create your own new PhpStorm tool based on this configuration and use it here, as shown in the following screenshot:

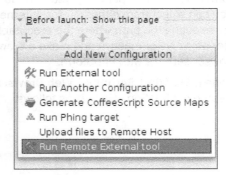

That's all there is to set your web application to be executed on a web server and viewed on a web browser. To execute web application code that you created, you need to right-click on the file in the editor and select **Open in browser**. Bingo!

Running your code

Having entered the world of PHP knowingly, you also stepped into the world of web programming as PHP is a popular web programming language too. An application written in PHP will have to be executed in either of the two mediums.

Getting ready

You need a web server such as Apache with the PHP module installed. If you need a web server, you are probably creating a web-based application that will run on a web browser.

How to do it...

To run PHP code, you need to learn just a shortcut *Ctrl + Shift + F10*. The rest is taken care of by PhpStorm.

The code will be executed according to the configuration you set. For more details about executing PHP code, you can refer to the previous chapter as well.

However, if you have no prior experience in executing PHP code in PhpStorm and you are not in the mood to try out something new, you can resort to old-school methods.

How it works...

You can use PhpStorm as the development system and the file transfer system to upload your code onto the web server where you can test the code there and then. The precondition is that the webserver should be a development server and that you just need to make changes to the PHP code only.

Does it not sound too old fashioned? Maybe. Read on.

If the development server is your local machine, this will be an inefficient way of doing things. In the case of your development server not being on your local machine, even if it is on the local network, there is a time lag involved in transferring files over the network. Being a developer, obviously you cannot afford to have this time lag unless the business requirements are such that you cannot have the entire system set up on your local machine.

[In all other cases, it is recommended that you have a local replica of the development server set up on your machine.]

Keep in pace with the new fashion. PhpStorm rocks!

4

Integrating Framework

In this chapter, we will cover the following topics:

- ▶ Cooking with Symfony
- ▶ Creating a controller with Symfony
- ▶ Creating a model with Symfony
- ▶ Creating a view with Symfony
- ▶ Creating a model with the Yii framework
- ▶ Creating a controller with the Yii framework
- ▶ Creating a view with the Yii framework
- ▶ Creating a model with the Zend framework
- ▶ Creating a controller with the Zend framework
- ▶ Creating a view with the Zend framework

Introduction

Before you start off, try some introspection as homework. Do you believe in reinventing the wheel? Do you believe in adding technical debt? If your answer to those questions was yes, you probably need to skip this chapter altogether. In all other cases, you should use a framework. Frameworks are good and nice with you. They help. They save time. They save effort.

Let's move back to questions. What is a technical debt? It is the amount of money at stake by a company where the technological architecture has been designed in such a way that more effort or man hours (and thus money) will be required to maintain the system in future. What is reinventing the wheel? It is the process of putting in more effort to carry out a task that was already done in the past.

Will you please stop scratching your head? This isn't rocket science. The analogy with software engineering is quite simple. You probably spend time in coding petty tasks, such as user input validation and password validation for each and every project that you create. While this is a repetition of tasks in the first place, it is the most vulnerable part of your code. The vulnerability is not only from general attackers, but also from certain very trivial mistakes, such as not cleaning the code.

You need to strategize your actions. This reinventing of the wheel is not free of cost. You are a highly paid developer (because you purchased a PhpStorm license (pun intended). Your billing agency will spend money to get work done by you. If you do work that is prone to errors, the billing agency will have to shell out more money to fix and/or maintain the same project later. Thus the agency is bound to spend money in the future and hence has a technical debt.

Please use a framework. You can take actions rapidly in building up chunks and pieces of your code using chunks and pieces from the framework. Your development process will be accelerated. You will be exposed to a library of functions for common tasks, database queries, and input cleaning, to name a few. The decision to choose a framework, however, needs a lot of thought.

There are still a few dangling questions that come to mind. You need to hold on and stay tuned for loads of important information. There are three frameworks that PhpStorm can be easily embedded with: Symfony, Yii, and Zend, in the lexicographic order of their names.

Cooking with Symfony

Symfony is a PHP web application framework for MVC applications available as free software and released under the MIT license.

To begin working with Symfony, you need to install Symfony on your local machine (also known as your local server). Life never lets you breathe easy. You have to choose from two (or more) paths to proceed. So is the case with PhpStorm.

Getting ready

Change often leads to confusion, so it is better to make few changes in the Symfony directory structure and jump to create a new controller. You create a new controller class inside the directory `<Project-Root>/src/Acme/DemoBundle/Controller`. Name it `CookingController.php`. Here are a few rules to follow:

- By default, you should create a controller with the suffix `Controller` in the name
- Each controller should extend the class `Controller` that is defined in the namespace `Symfony\Bundle\FrameworkBundle\Controller\Controller` namespace
- The controller should be defined in the namespace `Acme\DemoBundle\Controller`

Since you will require the routing of methods as actions, you will need to use namespace `Sensio\Bundle\FrameworkExtraBundle\Configuration\Route`.

You need to define a route in a configuration file (a file with the `.yml` extension) so that Symfony knows exactly where your controller is.

How to do it...

To install Symfony, you can choose from a simple archive download from the Symfony website or use Composer for installation. Composer? Yes, it's the same system that was described in *Chapter 2, PHP Development*, and some keywords to refresh your memory are composer.json, vendor directory, and so on.

Perform the following steps:

1. If you want to install Symfony by downloading it from the website, you need to go to `http://symfony.com/download`, select any of the archive formats, and download the archive to the disk.

2. Once the archive has been downloaded to the disk, you can move the unzipped directory inside your web server document root and open it in PhpStorm. There are two points worth noting:

    ❑ If you don't want the project to be web-based, you need not move it into the document root of your web server.

    ❑ If you want to create a web-based project, you can also keep the unzipped folders anywhere. You can then create a symbolic link inside your web server document root to point to this unzipped folder. This is to keep the system clean, you see.

To open the project in PhpStorm, you need to go to **File** | **Open** and open the path of the directory where you kept the Symfony directory.

The composer method is a bit long, but a careful PhpStorm cookbook reader need not worry because the information on how to use Composer was provided in *Chapter 2, PHP Development*. Perform the following steps:

1. You need to specify `symfony/framework-standard-edition` as the package name, as shown in the following screenshot. PhpStorm will show you the list of packages with similar names.

2. You need to specify the version number, and PhpStorm will be good to go. It will download the required dependencies for you.

[You should take care that you have a consistent Internet connection.]

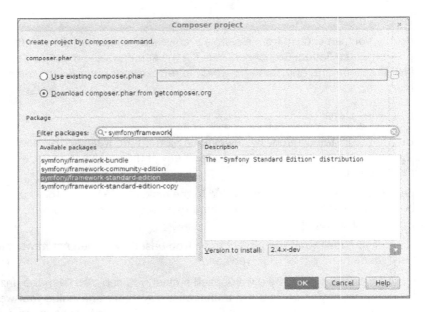

3. Once the framework has been downloaded, you can restart your IDE (not mandatory) to let PhpStorm breathe easy after doing the heavy-duty task of downloading the framework for you. As soon as you restart it, PhpStorm will be able to recognize which framework needs to be integrated. PhpStorm will guide you through integrating the framework usage.

4. You can tell PhpStorm about the directory and the type of content it will contain by providing the details. You just have to select some values from the dropdown, as shown in the following screenshot:

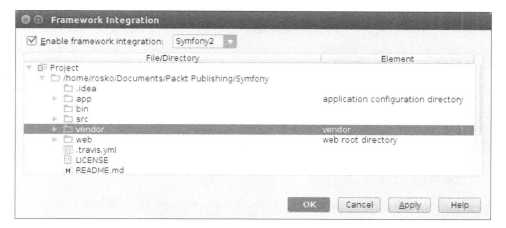

Thus, you are good to go with Symfony. There is a `readme.md` file provided at the project root level. You are encouraged to read it and follow the checklist that is provided with it.

How it works...

The Symfony framework adheres to the model-view-controller framework. Besides all the benefits that MVC serves, compartmentalizing the functionality is a major benefit. Thus, you will group all the database-related functions in the model, all the business logic in the controller, and all the presentation-related functions (generating the HTML) in the view. So, in order to dive deep into the details of Symfony, you need to understand the directory structure first.

There's more...

The directory structure is the basic skeleton of the project, and it is very important to know the directory structure before starting. Let's see the structure of Symfony.

Directory structure of Symfony

When you download and install Symfony, you are provided with a directory structure by default. There are five directories visible: the `app`, `bin`, `src`, `vendor`, and `web` directories.

The `app` folder is designed to contain the application-specific resources. These resources include the configurations for the database connections and the like in the `config` directory. The `logs` directory is intended to contain the logs to be written by the Symfony framework application. The cache directory is intended to contain the cached versions of files and resources required to run the application. A cached version is faster than the regular version and is write-protected. The resource directory is designed to contain resources such as the view rendering pages and the like.

The `bin` folder is designed to keep the binary files (such as `.sh`) that would be required by the project. The files under `bin` need to be executable because of their nature—to be able to be executed and perform the intended tasks independently. You need to be careful while providing execute permissions to files and folders.

The `src` folder is designed to contain the PHP source code required by the project. This PHP source code can be anything: your templates, classes, and anything you think is related to your project.

The `web` folder is designed to keep all the content that has to be rendered in a web browser over the Internet. This content includes HTML, JavaScript, CSS, images, icons, sprites, `robots.txt`, and so on, as and when required for the project.

The `vendor` directory is designed to keep all the third-party tools that are required for the project to run. This is an excellent feature because it keeps the third-party code in a separate compartment, thus protecting them from accidental edits.

It is worth noting here that a framework sets rules for you to work. If you stick to those rules, you will be on the winning side. One example supposes that there is the plugin X, which you downloaded from the Internet, a part of your code depends on it, and there is one `config` directory available for the project as a whole. There is a big chance that you might end up making changes or overwriting the `config` file. A framework will prevent you from doing that. How? It will indicate to you that a configuration inside the vendor directory must not be disturbed. If you still proceed to make changes intentionally or unintentionally, there is a limit to every warranty.

Mind you, "is designed to contain" means that it was the default intention. You can obviously store your classes wherever you want.

After you get yourself set on the directory structure, it is time to get your hands really dirty. Friends, Romans, Countrymen! Roll up your sleeves and do remember all that you shall see.

Inside the `app` folder, there is the `cache` folder. As already stated, it is used to cache some contents precooked so that they can be rendered very quickly. The caching can be done on commonly used elements, such as the images, strings, JavaScript, CSS, and certain preprocessed data. Since the PHP being executed on the web server writes the caches, the user running the web server (yes, you heard it right) needs permission to write into the `cache` folder. Exactly the same is true for the logs directory as well. You need to set permissions to the two folders mentioned as `777`. You can do even better. You can change the ownership of the two directories such that they are now owned by `www-data` or the Apache user (the username under the Linux environment). Try the `chown` or `chmod` command. Whatever you do, make sure you are doing it right. Ownership/permission changes are actions that can prove to be an issue, so don't do it when you feel sleepy.

Did you enjoy playing in the mud? More mud follows.

Go back to a point in history where you were really very hungry and were attempting to bake pizza using some cheese, salt, capsicum, and tomato (as a fallback topping). Remember? That was some freestyle cooking. What if you want more disciplined adventures in life? Try following the Symfony way.

Creating a controller with Symfony

So you will have to create a new controller first. This controller will be responsible for making decisions about how you will cook your Pizza.

Change often leads to confusion, so it is better to make few changes in the Symfony directory structure and just jump to create a new controller.

How to do it...

Create a new controller class inside the directory `<Project-Root>/src/Acme/DemoBundle/Controller`. Name it `CookingController.php`. There are a few rules to follow:

- By default, you should create a controller with the suffix `Controller` in the name
- Each controller should extend a class `Controller` that is defined in the namespace `Symfony\Bundle\FrameworkBundle\Controller\Controller`
- The controller should be defined in the namespace `Acme\DemoBundle\Controller`
- Since you will be required to route the methods as actions, you will need to use namespace `Sensio\Bundle\FrameworkExtraBundle\Configuration\Route`.
- You need to define a route in a configuration file (a file with the `.yml` extension) so that Symfony knows exactly where your controller is.

[You can define the route later.]

So, your first controller looks like the following code:

```
namespace Acme\DemoBundle\Controller;
use Symfony\Bundle\FrameworkBundle\Controller\Controller;
use Sensio\Bundle\FrameworkExtraBundle\Configuration\Route;
use Sensio\Bundle\FrameworkExtraBundle\Configuration\Template;
class CookingController extends Controller {
```

```
/**
 * @Route("/", name="_cooking")
 * @Template()
 */
public function indexAction() {
    return array();
}

/**
 * @Route("/nameDish/{dishname}", name="_cook_dish")
 * @Template()
 */
public function nameDishAction($dishname) {
return array('name' => $dishname);
}
}
```

And the content of the YML document (located at `<Project-root>/src/Acme/DemoBundle/Resources/config/routing.yml>`) will be (appended by):

```
_cook:
resource: "@AcmeDemoBundle/Controller/CookingController.php"
type: annotation
prefix: /cook
```

How it works...

The human mind is a very lazy machine. No sooner does it see any technical detail, than it starts getting confused. In order to eliminate the doubt, the working is explained here. Hang on. Begin with the source code because PHP is something you are more comfortable with. Here is the working.

The code starts with the declaration of a namespace that means you declared a virtual region or boundary for the elements of this controller. Technically, it is known as the namespace.

The code proceeds by including such namespaces for the base `Controller` and the routing system (denoted by `Route`).

If you want to include some presentation-layer templates, you can use the namespace of the templating engine as well. Twig is the name given to the default templating engine shipped with the default installation of Symfony.

Here, the most important aspect of a controller is that `CookingController` is a controller, so it is bound to extend the `Controller` class.

Inside the class are some simple methods that have public access. Did you say insecure? No, no dear! Since they are to be made available through a web browser, the access level has to be public.

The actual cooking starts by giving your dish a name. For this purpose, the method `nameDishAction` has the dish name as the parameter. Until now, things have been normal.

There is this annotation `@Route("/nameDish/{dishname}", name="_cook_dish")`, which adds the twist to the tale. `Route` creates a map between the action and the URL. This is another form of dependency injection. So, the name of the action `nameDish` is mapped with a name for the Symfony system (`_cook_dish`). If you look more closely, you will see that it also defines the way you will use this controller. The value specified in the braces is the placeholder for the argument that will be passed to this action.

Regarding the YML contents, it is worth mentioning that YML is actually YAML and is pronounced yamel. This is similar to any markup language with a key and its corresponding values. So, your resource will indicate the name of the controller you just created, the type your controller will be referenced as, and the prefix that will be required to be put with the actions as (to be) defined in your controller.

You just created a new Symfony controller to kick-start cooking. By the way, do you remember the last time you used the terminology dependency injection?

Creating a model with Symfony

How does an application remember things? Persistence is the name of the phenomenon by which any application maintains its state. To have persistence, you need to have data structure(s). To manage data structures in a typical engineering perspective, you can use models—the M in the MVC paradigm.

Getting ready

Remember that you have some toppings as well as some ingredients to be added to your pizza dish. So, typically, you need an array to store (represent) the toppings and the ingredients. This is a green signal to go ahead and use model. But again, there is a twist in the tale. Symfony has no default model system in place. Bad design? Maybe not. It was originally designed to be a request-response system. Symfony looks to you for this purpose. You can create a model freestyle.

How to do it...

1. Start by creating a new directory at the same level as the controller. Name it `Model`. This is descriptive naming, you see.

2. Inside the `Model` directory, use PhpStorm's new class wizard to create a new class. Name it `CookingModel.php`. It is not that Symfony will not accept anything other than `/*Model$/` in the class name.

3. You are encouraged to stick to names similar to the default Symfony names. Your model will look somewhat like the following code:

```php
namespace Acme\DemoBundle\Model;
use Doctrine\Common\CommonException;

class CookingModel {
  /**
    * Get the ingredients that will be added to your dish
    * @return array Containing the list of ingredients
  */
  public function getIngredients(){
    $ingredients = array('salt','cheese','');
    $ingredientCount = 0;
    try {
      while ($ingredientCount < count($ingredients)) {
        if ($ingredients[$ingredientCount] == '') {
          throw new CommonException("\nYou have run out of
capsicum.");
        }
        $ingredientCount++;
      }
    } catch (CommonException $e) {
      $ingredients[$ingredientCount] = 'tomato';
    }
    return $ingredients;
  }

  /**
    * Get the toppings that will be added to your dish
    * @return array Containing the list of toppings
  */

  public function getToppings(){
    return array('pepperoni','mushroom','onion','spinach');
  }
}
```

4. Since you just created a new model, the model will be of no use unless it is used inside a controller. Revisit `CookingController`. It had no action to actually cook a pizza. `Acme\DemoBundle\Model\CookingModel` should be appended to the controller file header. When you add the required action, you will do something like the following code:

```
/**
 * @Route("/startCooking/{dishname}",
name="_start_cooking_dish")
 * @Template()
 * @param string $dishname The name of the dish to be
cooked.
*/
public function startCookingAction($dishname){
  $items = new CookingModel();
  return array(
    'dishname' => $dishname,
    'ingredients' => $items->getIngredients(),
    'toppings' => $items->getToppings()
  );
}
```

How it works...

Now that you already have some experience in cooking, the model class is quite simple. If you recall, the content of the model is just a smart copy-paste from the `PizzaDish` class.

The namespace for the `CommonException` class was used to catch some exceptions if they occurred while cooking. This is safe cooking indeed.

The `getIngredients` method processes the available ingredients and returns an array containing the ingredients. It also prevents your pizza from becoming unenjoyable without capsicum—it adds tomato as a fallback ingredient.

The `getToppings` method functions similarly. It provides a list of the toppings you would like to add to make your pizza yummier.

Inside the controller, the model is used just like any other class. Inside the `startCookingAction`, all you did was create a new model object and obtain the value from the model.

Even simpler! So, you created a new model in Symfony. Congratulations! You can safely gobble up the pizza you just baked (or cooked—mind you, you are an engineer and not a cook, so the difference between cooking and baking should not bother you).

Creating a view with Symfony

You can skip this section if you have planned to use Symfony to create a command-line software. But if you want to write software where you need to show beautiful presentation, you need to follow this section very carefully. The face of your application is known as view.

Getting ready

You need to create views in a particular directory if you stick to the default Symfony settings. The name of the directory in the present installation is `<Project-root>/symfony/src/Acme/DemoBundle/Resources/views`. You also have to create a directory that contains the name of the controller minus the word `controller`. Thus, you will create a directory with the name `Cooking` as you created a controller with the name `CookingController`.

How to do it...

While naming the file, you have to keep in mind that you will name the view file with the extension `.html.twig`, and the filename will be the same as the name of the action minus `Action`, which will render the view.

So, you can have views with the name `index.html.twig`, `nameDish.html.twig`, and `startCooking.html.twig` as you created `indexAction`, `nameDishAction`, and `startCookingAction`, respectively.

By this time, you must be asking what bird **TWIG** is. You must also be thinking about starting to curse the author for having provided so much information. Dear, dear, dear. Art is long and life is short. Twig is a templating engine for PHP. It is designed to inject dynamic behavior into HTML pages. This is especially helpful for user interface developers who have little knowledge about the server-side language, which renders the HTML onto a web browser. Assuming you have to create a view, you will do something like this for `startCookingAction`:

```
<!DOCTYPE html>
<html>
<head>
<title>Let us cook {{ dishname }}</title>
<style type="text/css">
.align-center{
  text-align: center;
}
.heading{
  font-weight: bold;
  font-size: 40px;
}
```

```
.normal-text{
  font-size: 16px;
}
</style>
</head>
<body>
<div class="align-center heading">You are now cooking {{ dishname
}}!</div>
<div class="align-center normal-text">By adding ingredients
{% for key, ingredient in ingredients %}
| {{ ingredient }}
{% endfor %}
</div>
<div class="align-center normal-text">And toppings
{% for key, topping in toppings %}
| {{ topping }}
{% endfor %}
</div>
</body>
</html>
```

The immediate remedy for the visual injury caused to you just now is to explain to you how this code works. An overview of this code is that it is for an HTML page.

How it works...

Inside the HTML `title` tag, there is `{{ dishname }}`, which is the dynamic content. If you revisit the method `startCookingAction` inside `CookingController`, you will notice that you returned an array with the index `dishname`. The placeholder `dishname` assumes its value from the controller action. If the controller returns an array, you will obviously require iterating the entire array to use the values in the view. A for-loop begins and ends with `for` and `endfor` respectively. Thus, the loop iterates over the array returned from the controller (`$ingredients` and `$toppings`) with the array index as key and the array values as the ingredient and topping respectively. The values thus obtained (ingredient and topping respectively) are used in the view.

You just cooked your pizza using a new method. Do you love it? There is no pun intended here.

Creating a model with the Yii framework

The roadmap begins with creating a model. Then, create a controller and use the model you created. Finally, give a face to your application by creating a view. Use the model to get data and pass it on to the view.

How to do it...

Creating a new model is extremely easy. It is no different to creating a simple PHP class in PhpStorm. To create a new model, you need to create a new PHP class inside `<project-root>/app/models`. Your model will look like the following code:

```php
namespace app\models;
class Cooking {
  /**
    * Get the ingredients that will be added to your dish
    * @return array Containing the list of ingredients
  */
  public function getIngredients(){
    $ingredients = array('salt','cheese','');
    $ingredientCount = 0;
    try {
      while ($ingredientCount < count($ingredients)) {
        if ($ingredients[$ingredientCount] == '') {
          throw new \ErrorException("\nYou have run out of
capsicum.");
        }
        $ingredientCount++;
      }
    } catch (\ErrorException $e) {
      $ingredients[$ingredientCount] = 'tomato';
    }
    return $ingredients;
  }
  public function getToppings(){
    return array('pepperoni','mushroom','onion','spinach');
  }
}
```

How it works...

This model is exactly the same as the model you created in Symfony. Remember? The namespace of the model is declared so that any other class is able to access the methods defined in the model.

The exception available is defined in the `ErrorException` class, so it is used to handle the exception.

 This is why they say that your business logic is what really matters. So, irrespective of the framework, your data class (the model) remained the same.

Creating a controller with the Yii framework

To create a new controller, create a new PHP class inside the controller folder. Name it `CookingController.php`. The reason for this? You have been doing this for a while now, so you should continue doing it lest your stomach gets angry. Keep cooking, comrade.

How to do it...

To create a new controller, go to a new PHP class. Use the name `CookingController.php`. Do remember the directory `<project-root>/app/controllers`. Your controller will look somewhat like the following code:

```
namespace app\controllers;

use app\models\Cooking;
use Yii;
use yii\web\Controller;

class CookingController extends Controller
{
  public function actionIndex(){
    $items = new Cooking();
    $dishname = 'pizza';
    $ingredients = $items->getIngredients();
    $toppings = $items->getToppings();
    return $this>render('index',array('dishname'=>$dishname,
    'ingredients'=>$ingredients,'toppings' => $toppings));
  }
}
```

How it works...

On careful examination of the controller, you will have mixed feelings. You will be able to see some known-to-you elements in the code and some new elements.

The namespace of the controller is declared as `app\controllers`. This means that if some other controller needs to use the methods (actions) defined in this controller, that controller will have to use this namespace.

Since the data is being fetched from the model you created, in order to use the model's methods, you need to use the namespace in which the model is declared.

You need to use the namespace where the parent controller (defined by the framework) is defined.

The controller contains an action `actionIndex`. In Yii, the actions defined follow this naming convention: the word `action` followed by the actual purpose of the action. Thus, the `actionIndex` will be the default action for the controller.

The action requires a view as well. It is called by the method render: the first argument being the name of the view and the other argument the list of values to be passed on from the controller to the view.

Creating a view with the Yii framework

Now, create a view to make your application complete. In creating a new view, you need to be careful.

How to do it...

The proper location of a view in a project is the `<project-root>/views/<first-name-of-the-controller>` directory. Thus, you will require a new directory under the views. Create a new directory with the name `cooking`. Inside this directory, create a new PHP file with the name `index.php`. Having done that, you need to write some basic HTML code to make a view. You might write something like the following code:

```php
<?php
use yii\helpers\Html;
$this->title = 'Let us cook ';
?>
<!DOCTYPE html>
<html >
<head>
<head>
<meta charset="<?= Yii::$app->charset ?>"/>
<title><?= Html::encode($this->title).$dishname ?></title>
<style type="text/css">
.align-center{text-align: center;}
.heading {font-weight: bold;font-size: 40px;}
.normal-text {font-size: 16px;}
</style>
</head>
</head>
<body>

<div class="align-center heading">You are now cooking <?php echo
$dishname; ?>!</div>
<div class="align-center normal-text">By adding ingredients
<?php
```

```
foreach($ingredients as $ingredient){
  ?> | <?php
  echo $ingredient;
}
?>
</div>
<div class="align-center normal-text">And toppings
<?php
foreach($toppings as $topping){
  ?> | <?php
  echo $topping;
}
?>
</div>
</body>
</html>
```

How it works...

The `html` part in the code is standard and does not use any other framework. The CSS is also kept basic to keep the code readable and simple to understand. When you use the namespace `YII/helpers/HTML`, it brings to your control the HTML helper class that performs basic HTML operations, such as encoding the input that might contain some special characters into HTML entities, and so on. The framework sets the charset (the character set) to be used on the web page.

The data that you passed on from the controller is now available in your view. The variable name is the name of the array index that you passed, and the value of the variable is the array value that was set at that array index. Thus, you will have `$dishname`, `$ingredients`, and `$toppings` in your view. In order to display the contents of the array, you just need to do a simple PHP `foreach` to iterate over the array, and your cooking process will be complete.

 It is not only `foreach` that will do the trick—you can use whichever loop control structure you like.

Creating a model with the Zend framework

You will require a new model to make all the ingredients and the toppings available. Then, you would require a controller that would be the entry point for your application, and which would control the cooking process. To wrap up things, you require a view to which you will pass on the data from the controller, and your cooking will conclude.

How to do it...

This time, creating a new model is not at all difficult.

You just need to create a new PHP class inside the `<project-root>/module/` `Application/src/Application/Model` directory in just the same way as you have done all the while.

Name it `Cooking`, and set the namespace as `Application\Model`. The purpose of your model class will be to supply the ingredients to facilitate the cooking process.

Your model will look somewhat like the following code:

```php
namespace Application\Model;
class Cooking {
  /**
    * Get the ingredients that will be added to your dish
    * @return array Containing the list of ingredients
  */
  public function getIngredients(){
    $ingredients = array( 'salt','cheese', '' );

    $ingredientCount = 0;
    try {
      while ($ingredientCount < count($ingredients)) {
        if ($ingredients[$ingredientCount] == '') {
          throw new \ErrorException("\nYou have run out of
capsicum.");
        }
        $ingredientCount++;
      }
    } catch (\ErrorException $e) {
      $ingredients[$ingredientCount] = 'tomato';
    }
    return $ingredients;
  }
  public function getToppings(){
    return array( 'pepperoni', 'mushroom', 'onion', 'spinach' );
  }
}
```

How it works...

The model is quite easy to understand because if you are careful enough and possess a reasonable memory, you will easily recall that the model is exactly the same. The only difference here is the exception-handling class. Zend provides `ErrorException` to handle common exceptions.

You must feel better by now since you created a model quite easily.

Creating a controller with the Zend framework

Now's the time to create a new controller. To do that, you will have to perform the following steps:

1. Create a new class inside `<project root>/module/Application/src/Application/Controller`.

2. Name it `CookingController`, and set the namespace `Application\Controller`.

3. Use the namespace for the model since you need the model's methods in your code.

4. Use the namespace for `AbstractActionController` as you need to tell Zend that your controller is `AbstractActionController`.

5. Use the namespace for `ViewModel` since you will need to render a view when you run the code. Your controller will look like the following code:

```
namespace Application\Controller;

use Application\Model\Cooking;
use Zend\Mvc\Controller\AbstractActionController;
use Zend\View\Model\ViewModel;
class CookingController extends AbstractActionController {
  public function indexAction() {
    $dishname = 'Pizza';
    $items = new Cooking();
    $renderView = new ViewModel(
      array('dishname' => $dishname,'ingredients' =>
$items->getIngredients(),
    'toppings' => $items->getToppings()));
    $renderView->setTerminal(true);
    return $renderView;
  }
}
```

How it works...

The code that you wrote just now is a controller class that uses some other classes to make things work as per your requirements. Thus, the typical thing that you might have noticed is the `ViewModel` method. The `ViewModel` method is actually a constructor method to the class `ViewModel` defined in the namespace `Zend\View\Model\ViewModel`. The purpose of this method is to render the view and pass on some values from the controller if need be. The `setTerminal` method that belongs to the `ViewModel` class prevents any other layout from rendering in your view. Without this, the framework looks for a `layout.phtml` file somewhere, which will render the general layout of the view component. Thus, your entire presentation will reside inside the `index.phtml` file that you will create next.

Creating a view with the Zend framework

Having created the controller and the model, you can proceed to create a view and give your application a face.

How to do it...

1. Go to the `<project-root>/module/Application/view/application/cooking` directory, create a new PHP file, and name it `index.phtml`.

    Phtml is a special extension used in the Zend framework that tells the web server that the expected content in the file will be more HTML and less PHP.

    In other words, it is a way to tell the server that the file is a view component. Just as you have been doing all this while to create a view, you will take similar actions this time as well. After all, a view is a view.

2. You will create something like the following code:

    ```
    <?php echo $this->doctype(); ?>
    <html lang="en">
    <head>
    <?php echo $this->headTitle('Let us cook '.$dishname)-
    >setSeparator(' - ')->setAutoEscape(false) ?>
    </head>
    ```

    Now we've defined the title. Let's move to other parts of the code, which are as follows:

    ```
    <style type="text/css">
    .align-center{ text-align: center; }
    .heading{ font-weight: bold; font-size: 40px; }
    .normal-text{ font-size: 16px; }
    </style>
    ```

3. A simple-to-understand piece of CSS to garnish the recipes is as follows:

```
<body>
<div class="align-center heading">You are now cooking <?php echo
$dishname; ?>!</div>
<div class="align-center normal-text">By adding ingredients
<?php
foreach($ingredients as $ingredient){
  ?> | <?php
  echo $ingredient;
}?>
</div>
<div class="align-center normal-text">and toppings
<?php
foreach($toppings as $topping){
  ?> | <?php
  echo $topping;
}?>
</div>
</body>
</html>
```

How it works...

The HTML part is quite simple. The difference is in the following two points:

▶ `$this->doctype()`: This is a method in the `Zend\View\Renderer\
PhpRenderer` class that sets the `doctype` declaration for an HTML page

▶ `$this->headTitle($title)`: This is a method in the same class that sets the
title of a page as `$title`. The remaining part is exactly the same in terms of usage.

Details! Thunderbolt! Your pizza still won't be cooked. You will have to work more in the Zend
framework. It's time to move to the *There's more...* section to bake your incomplete pizza.

There's more...

You need to create a configuration related to your application module. Inside `<Project-
root>/module/Application/config`, create a new PHP file with the name `module.
config.php`. You need to tell the Zend framework about the routes, the controllers, and the
views that you will use to cook the pizza.

Your efforts can take the following shape:

```
return array('router' => array('routes' => array('home' =>
array('type' =>'Zend\Mvc\Router\Http\Literal', 'options' =>
array('route' => '/', 'defaults' => array('controller' =>
'Application\Controller\Cooking', 'action' => 'index', ),),),),),
'controllers' => array( 'invokables' => array(
'Application\Controller\Cooking'
=>'Application\Controller\CookingController'),),
'view_manager' => array( 'template_path_stack' => array( __DIR__ .
'/../view',),),),);
```

A router contains routes. Routes contain the home route. The home route contains the type of route and routing options. The routing options contain the route and the default values, such as the controller name and the action name. Thus, you will want your `CookingController` to be active by default and the `indexAction` to take place by default.

The controllers contain the name that you want Zend to know your controller by. Actually, the name that Zend remembers your controllers by are through their class names minus the `Controller` word. Thus Zend will invoke your controller by the settings you specify for the inviolable.

Having created a view, you will want to tell Zend where your view files are. Inside, the `view_manager` does the same by setting the path of the template (`template_path_stack`).

Still some work remains. Oh God! When will the pizza get cooked? God says: "Be patient and be honest. You will enjoy."

You have to create a new PHP class inside `<Project-root>/module/Application` (with the name `Module`) so that you are able to use the routing and the related settings for your module. Your `Module.php` file will look somewhat like the following code:

```
namespace Application;
class Module {
  public function getConfig(){
  return include __DIR__ . '/config/module.config.php';
}

public function getAutoloaderConfig() {
  return array(
    'Zend\Loader\StandardAutoloader' => array(
      'namespaces' => array(
      __NAMESPACE__ => __DIR__ . '/src/' . __NAMESPACE__,
),),),);
  }
}
```

You need to stick to the Zend system to make things right and standard. To use module-specific configurations, you use the settings inside the `getConfig` method. In order to tell Zend where the classes to be included for execution are, you need to use `getAutoloaderConfig`.

Now you can say that you created the pizza successfully. You can now sit back on your couch and enjoy the taste. If you did not quite like the taste, there is always a next time!

5

Testing and Debugging

In this chapter, we will cover the following topics:

- ▶ Installing PHPUnit
- ▶ Test case in PHPUnit
- ▶ Testing an application with PHPUnit
- ▶ Starting a debugging session
- ▶ Setting a breakpoint
- ▶ Configuring breakpoint conditions
- ▶ Creating exception breakpoints
- ▶ Stepping through your code
- ▶ Running to a line of code selected
- ▶ Watching expressions and variables
- ▶ Evaluating expressions
- ▶ Changing code on the fly
- ▶ Code coverage in PhpStorm

Introduction

Whenever you create a new software, there is a business dependency inherent on that. Obviously, if your software were not sold, you would probably have opted for some other profession. Due to the business factor, you are always expected to make your software reliable. This can be done only after your software has passed testing. It is not that you, the programmers, will do the entire testing and kick the tester out. You will be required to do the unit testing while actually writing the code. If you unit test your code, the chances of failure decrease drastically. The unit testing should ideally be done while creating code, and an ideal timeline to unit test is as soon as some milestone functionality has been created.

To act wisely and do (unit) testing, use PHPUnit. **PHPUnit** is a system (application) written in your favorite PHP. It lets you write test cases for the code you write so that you can keep on checking for any error that might creep into your logic. Thus, by the time you use a build tool to create something like a phar or any other archive, you have already ensured that the first level of filtration has been applied.

It is obvious for you to ask the purpose of PHPUnit then. The answer to this is simple: you need PHPUnit to prevent errors from passing on to the integration testing phase. But what if there were some errors or functionality that could not be detected at the unit-testing phase? What if there were errors due to another component or module passing on erroneous data?

Instead of applying the same rule to change the tense of a person's existence, you are again advised to act wisely. Use a debugger. Most of the IDEs show debugger with a bug icon next to it, so you would not find it difficult to find it in PhpStorm. PhpStorm provides you with options to select a debugger and integrate it for usage.

Using a debugger, you can do wonders. You actually gain fine-grained control over your code. You gain the power to walk across walls and see through iron plates! Will you stop dreaming about being a superpower, please. You are still a software engineer? A debugger gives you the power to look into the value of any variable in your code and the return value of a method, to pause the execution at will and resume it at will, and the list is endless.

Before diving into the deep sea of knowledge, it is important to know the difference between testing and debugging. **Testing** is a process that is likely to be done during the development phase, just after some business logic has been developed and it needs to be cleaned and sanitized properly before being released into production. **Debugging** is the process of removal of bugs from the code. A bug is that unwanted (improper) functionality that has passed the testing phase and has been discovered in the later testing phases or even in the production phase. Actually, both are similar because the aim of both is just to clean the product and functional software application.

Installing PHPUnit

The discussion starts with testing because it precedes debugging in the software development life cycle. PHP provides a unit-testing system, which is known as PHPUnit.

Getting ready

If you use PHPUnit, you gain the freedom to write some code and to check some code. Yes, you read it right. You can use PHPUnit to write some program that will check the input and output of some other program. Interesting phenomenon, right?

When you can write an application (PHP code) using an application (PhpStorm), why not test the application (PHP code) with an application (PHPUnit test cases)? Since PHPUnit is just an application written in PHP, it is available in the form of a **PHP Archive** (**PHAR**). It is just a method to ship your files and folders as a whole and to make it ready to be executed.

 Please make sure that you have PHP interpreter installed before installing PHPUnit.

How to do it...

You can install it very easily by just downloading the PHPUnit archive (the `phar` file) and setting the `/path/to/phpunit.phar` in the list of include paths.

You just need to perform the following steps:

1. Go to the **Project** view.
2. Access the right-click context menu on the **External Libraries** directory.
3. Select the **Configure PHP includes path** option.

You can also do that quickly by selecting the **External Libraries** directory, pressing *F4*, and pointing to the correct `phpunit.phar` file, as shown in the following screenshot:

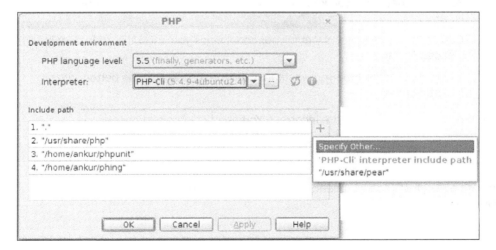

How it works...

Since you have installed PHPUnit as a package (PHAR), the testing system swings into action as soon as you inherit (or extend) a class defined inside the directory `phpunit-lts.phar` under the `phpunit` directory and the framework subdirectory with the name `PHPUnit_Framework_TestCase`.

Test case in PHPUnit

Having installed PHPUnit successfully, your challenge is not over yet—it has just led to another array of challenges. Testing is no easy task, but it is interesting. Just as you love writing beautiful PHP code, you will love writing test cases in PHPUnit because it is just like writing PHP code while taking care of some conventions.

A **test case** is a piece of an application that is written specifically to check (or test) for certain conditions in another application. Thus, when you write down a test case, you actually write a PHP code to test if something has gone wrong in other PHP code (which happens to be the code you have written to meet the business requirements).

Here, it is quite important to state that you, the programmer, usually have the following point of view:

- ▶ You think that since you know your code very well you know that your code is errorless
- ▶ Even if there are some errors in your code, since you know the code deeply, you can fix it in a flash
- ▶ You think that the time you waste in writing test cases can be better utilized in writing more code

These (and many such) points are incorrect. You need to write test cases.

How to do it...

To create a new test case, you need to create a new PHPUnit class. Thus, perform the following steps:

1. Go to the **Project** view.
2. Select the file you want to test. This file should be a valid PHP class. Obvious statement.

3. From the right-click context menu, select **New | PHPUnit | PHPUnit Test**, as shown in the following screenshot:

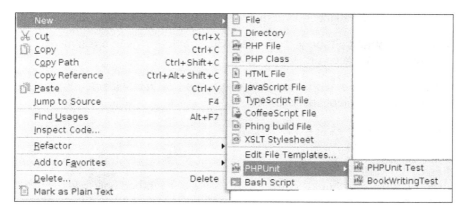

4. Provide the name and the related details just as you would do to create a new PHP class.

 The test cases that you create will be PHP methods with the public access specifier inside this class.

How it works...

To see how a test case works, you need to follow some conventions. The reason is that, since a test case is a PHP code, it has to have some functionality inherent in it. The conventions are listed for quick reference:

▶ The test class should have the same name as the target class. Thus, you will create XXXTest inside the file XXXTest.php given that the name of the class to be tested is XXX.

▶ All test classes should extend (inherit) the PHPUnit_Framework_TestCase class. This class is made available to you when you include the PHAR in your PhpStorm project (as we saw in the *Installing PHPUnit* recipe of this chapter).

Thus, your class XXXTest will have the following declaration:

```
class XXXTest extends PHPUnit_Framework_TestCase{
..
}
```

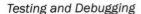

The exact method to be tested inside the test class should have its name starting with `test` followed by the name of the method to be tested.

It is not that your test will fail just due to this reason, but it is a standard naming practice.

There is also no constraint on you to map one-to-one test methods to one single target method. Again, it is just a good practice.

Thus, given that the name of the method to be tested is `YYY`, a test inside your test class will have the declaration (definition) as follows:

```
public function testYYY(){
    ...
}
```

As per the convention, you should write one test inside one method only. It leads to better organization of code and makes it easier to understand.

The actual testing is done by asserting some facts. The facts are the output of the methods you will be testing. Thus, if some method returns a string, you can check if the method return type is `string` by writing the following line of code:

```
$this->assertInternalType("string", $methodReturnValue);
```

A test class should have the common content inside a `setUp` method. This is particularly helpful in cases in which you need to have a chunk of code shared across all the test methods in this class. It is your call whether to use it or not.

At the end of a test method being called, you might not need to have the resources at hand. You might want to remove it from memory.

Here, it is quite important to remember that you should always design your tests wisely. You should always prevent unwanted memory usage in your test because once you do that, you will have to add another testing on this test class as well.

Having known the nuances of test cases, you are all set to test. This is a deliberate misuse of the letters of the alphabet to alert you!

Whatever you do, PhpStorm assists you. So, instead of waiting and thinking about what to do, get set, go!

Testing an application with PHPUnit

There must be a question hovering in your mind about the role of PhpStorm in this testing. It's time for action. Having sufficient knowledge of the conventions to write tests, you can proceed to face the real world of testing. The more you test, the purer your code will become. Testing is good. Testing is healthy. Testing is recommended.

How to do it...

Good question. This question is best answered with some diving back into time to get back the same pizza cooking use case. You have grown up listening to grandma's advice to reuse objects. Now is the time for you to reuse. Perform the following steps:

1. Reuse the `PizzaDish` class. You will create a test class somewhat like the following:

```php
require_once "PizzaDish.php";
class PizzaDishTest extends PHPUnit_Framework_TestCase {

  function setUp(){
    $this->pizzaDish = new PizzaDish("Pizza Dish", "Dish");
  }

  function tearDown(){
    unset($this->pizzaDish);
  }

  public function testGetInstance(){
    $this->assertInstanceOf('Dish',
    $this->pizzaDish->getInstance());
  }

  public function testGetDishName(){
    $this->assertInternalType("string",
    $this->pizzaDish->getDishName());
  }
}
```

As promised, you can see that the PHPUnit is all about writing PHP classes.

2. To execute this test, you need to execute (run) this class.

3. Running this class is extremely simple. *Ctrl + Shift + F10* is your savior.

4. If you want to run a single method, PhpStorm provides for that as well. You just need to place the cursor anywhere inside the body of the method you want to execute and issue the run command.

 If the cursor is not inside a method body, the entire test class will be executed.

The following screenshot shows the test result:

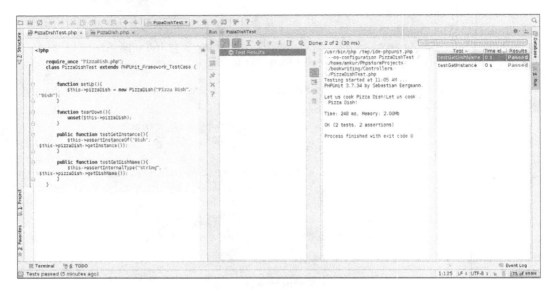

How it works...

In order to execute your unit test, PhpStorm makes some improvisations. Just as it does with every other library, it uses its own version of the execution script to execute the test. The full name of the file is /tmp/ide-phpunit.php. Thus, it is this file that accepts the name of the test class file you have written.

The working of the testing application is simple. As already stated, all classes that inherit PHPUnit_Framework_TestCase class become test classes. The setUp method instantiates an object of the target class PizzaDish and makes it available to the entire test class.

Inside your test class, the testGetInstance and testGetDishName methods get executed when you run the test. Inside the test method, a new object is instantiated to initiate the actual testing process. Up until this point, the activities that you did were the same as those for a PHP class. Inside the methods, there are certain assertions that do the actual testing. There are these special methods, namely, assertInstanceOf and assertInternalType, which are declared in the Assert class provided by the framework. You can view the documentation of the method by putting the cursor under the method name and pressing *Ctrl + Q*. These are the actual methods that perform the testing task by checking if the given assertion is true. Thus, the motive of the test class that you created is to check whether the desired class is instantiated or not and whether the name of the dish that you want to cook is of the type string.

Once you run the test, you will be able to see the test results in the usual run view which is accessible by *Alt + 4*.

Starting a debugging session

"Now is the time for all programmers to start debugging their code"

Like most IDEs, PhpStorm also uses a bug icon to show the debugger. Just as a bug leeches your blood and doesn't let you concentrate on your main task, a software bug can leech precious CPU cycles and not allow your software to work as expected.

To prevent such bugs from entering the life cycle of software, you need to do debugging. Debugging is the process of diving deep into the code and finding out the potential areas that might be the problem causing regions in the code, so do extensive lookup to find and rectify the bugs.

The tools available for the purpose are termed debuggers in the industry. **Xdebug** is the name for one such tool. It is a very commonly used, free, and open source debugger that is available to be plugged in with most IDEs.

Getting ready

To plug it in, you need to install it on your development machine. Perform the following steps:

1. Check out the source code from **GitHub**, the repository where Xdebug is hosted. You need to issue this command in your terminal `git clone git://github.com/xdebug/xdebug.git`.

2. Move into the directory where the code has been checked out.

3. Issue the command `phpize`. There will be lots of text output to the console when you do this. Once the output finishes, you need to execute the configuration file, which happens to be an executable shell script.

4. You need to enable `xdebug` using the switch `--enable-xdebug` while configuring. Thus, you should write `./configure --enable-xdebug`.

5. When this has been done, you need to issue the command `make && make install` to complete the compilation.

6. The output of steps will be a module—precisely a shared object or a `.so` file that you need to specify in the PHP settings. Kindly note it.

7. Inside the appropriate `ini` file, you need to write the following code:

```
zend_extension="/path/to/compiled/xdebug/so/xdebug.so"
xdebug.remote_enable=On
xdebug.remote_host=localhost
xdebug.remote_port=9000
```

8. In order to know which `php.ini` file your PhpStorm uses, you need to go to **Tools | Run Command** and issue the command `php --ini`. You will be given a list of all the `.ini` files that are parsed. You now have the correct `.ini` file to make the changes in.

There is this shortcut as well, *Ctrl + Shift + X*, which opens the command-line tool console.

Having installed a powerful debugger, you can proceed to making your code bug-free.

How to do it...

A debugging session is to be started only for a web-based PHP application. In order to be able to initiate the debugging for a web application, perform the following steps:

1. You need to have, let's say for Chrome, an `xdebug` helper. It helps you to initiate a debugging session once you type in a URL.

2. You know that corresponding to a client, there should be a server so that when you attempt to initiate a debug session, there must have been a listener for the incoming connection.

3. So, you need to start the listener for the incoming debug connection. To do that, you need to go to **Run | Start Listen to debug connections**.

4. Once you initiate the session for the first time, PhpStorm shows an alert regarding some entry, as shown in the screenshot following the next information box:

Make sure that the checkbox is checked for **Can accept external connection**. This will be found in **Settings | PHP | Debug**.

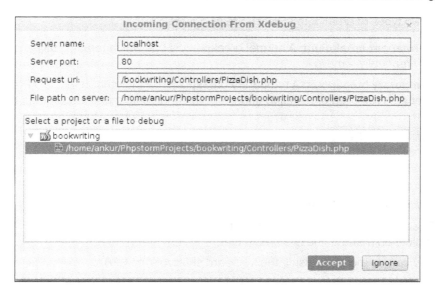

How it works...

Once you accept the connection, PhpStorm saves it. The saved servers can be viewed later under **File | Settings | PHP | Servers**. From this point onwards, the debugging process becomes the same for a web-based application and a command-line application. So the debugger will view whatever variables will be there in the code, and according to the breakpoints that you provide, it will pause, continue, step through, or step over the code, thus making it very easy for you to see what is going on inside the code.

> You can also visit `http://www.xdebug.org/wizard.php` to know more about `xdebug` installation for your server.

Setting a breakpoint

A breakpoint in a code is that point (or line of code) where you want the program execution to pause for a while. When you were cooking pizza and adding ingredients, suppose you wanted to know at any instant which ingredient was about to be added, you can set a breakpoint to actually make the interpreter pause at the line where the variable contained the name of the ingredient to be added. After a breakpoint is set, you can see which value a variable assumes under the variables frame in the debug window.

There are two types of breakpoints, which are as follows:

▶ **Permanent breakpoint**: A normal breakpoint is one which remains till eternity, until you manually remove it

▶ **Temporary breakpoint**: A temporary breakpoint, on the other hand, is a breakpoint that gets removed or disabled upon certain conditions, the most common being a hit.

How to do it...

1. To set a normal breakpoint, you need to select a suspicious line of code by placing the cursor under it.

2. Go to **Run | Toggle Line Breakpoint**.

3. There will be a red circle created at the left-hand side panel to give you a visual indication that the line is a breakpoint.

4. You can do the same using the keyboard shortcut *Ctrl + F8*.

How it works...

A breakpoint allows you to view the state of the variables stack. So, when the interpreter halts at a breakpoint, you can view the contents of the variables involved in the program execution. If you have added some variables or expressions to *watch*, you can constantly view the content of the selected variable at all times as long as it remains in the current scope. At all other times during the execution, there is the message **Cannot evaluate expression** shown. The debugger provides instruction to the interpreter to pause the execution when a breakpoint is hit. Upon request, the debugger instructs the interpreter to write (output) messages to the console (and it appears to the human eye that PhpStorm has done it!)

Configuring breakpoint conditions

PhpStorm provides you ways to customize the breakpoints. So you have some more comfort to sit back and enjoy the debugging happening, while being sure that your task will be done in time.

How to do it...

1. Once you set a breakpoint, you can press *Ctrl + Shift + F8* to get a configuration panel. Using the panel, you can change the regular breakpoint to a temporary breakpoint.

2. Select the checkbox next to the **Remove once hit** option. That breakpoint will only be existent till the breakpoint is hit once.

3. You can select **Log message to console** to output once this breakpoint gets hit.

4. You can create an expression to be evaluated once this breakpoint gets hit by selecting the **Log evaluated expression** checkbox. You can also keep this breakpoint dormant conditionally.

5. You can tell PhpStorm to activate this breakpoint to remain disabled until an exception of a particular type is thrown, as shown in the following screenshot:

How it works...

Again, there is no logical explanation as to how a breakpoint works. You need to follow the steps shown, and PhpStorm will do the trick for you. The working is more related to the operating system.

 While the pop up is still open, you can press *Ctrl + Shift + F8* to get a larger panel in which you can have a peek into the code as well, while still having the control panel open.

This is as shown in the following screenshot:

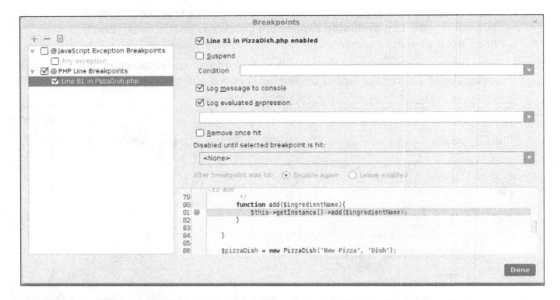

Creating exception breakpoints

There is new information for your brain to absorb. Until this point in time, you assumed that a breakpoint can be created only manually when you suspected some line of code might be problematic. But you can actually create a breakpoint to be hit when an exception is hit. This type of breakpoint is known as **exception breakpoint**. The question that comes to mind is "what is the reason for this name?" This breakpoint gets activated on encountering an exception.

How to do it...

To create a new exception breakpoint, you just need to remember a few small steps:

1. Inside the editor, press *Ctrl + Shift + F8*, where there will be a pop up.

2. In the left-hand top corner, there is the **+** sign, press it and you will get an option to create an exception breakpoint.

3. On proceeding, you will be asked to enter the name of the exception at which you want the execution to halt.

4. You can also make a customization in the way the breakpoint will behave. You can ask PhpStorm to activate this breakpoint when an unexpected (or uncaught) exception is thrown in the code, as shown in the following screenshot. This is particularly helpful for a wise programmer since most of the expected exceptions will have already been covered in the code. All the other rules that were applicable on a general breakpoint are applicable on the exception breakpoint except for this one difference.

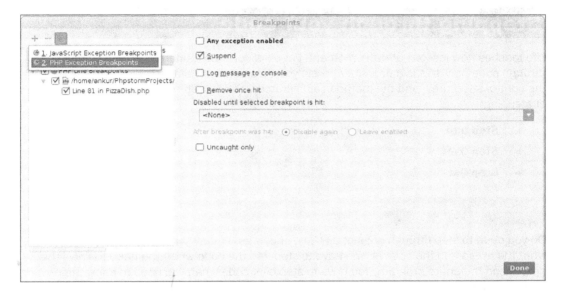

 You cannot disable an exception breakpoint once it is hit. In other words, you cannot make a temporary exception breakpoint.

5. If you want the exception breakpoint to be activated upon some condition, you can leave the exception disabled until either another exception occurs or another breakpoint is hit. PhpStorm provides you with the options to choose from a list of breakpoints for the purpose.

 To avoid laboring hard in making the decision as to which exception to choose, you can select the exception to be the Exception class. This can prove handy because all the exception classes ultimately inherit this Exception class.

How it works...

The execution continues in the normal way—if you have set breakpoints, there will be pauses as there used to be. But now, the execution will pause on an exception as well. Thus, this exception breakpoint is an invisible breakpoint that will not be visible to you, but internally it will be active. Being a breakpoint, it will continue working as a breakpoint.

Stepping through your code

Life teaches new lessons at every moment. For all of you who found the phrase *stepping through code* new, this is a process wherein you do an analysis of the values of variables, the control structures, and the method call hierarchy. The process includes three types of stepping:

- **Step Into**
- **Step Over**
- **Step Out**

Getting ready

Do you need to step through code at all? Yes, of course. When? When you have to find out what the eyesore in the code is. You have to step into the code when you need to know the next line in the entire program. You have to step over code when you need to know the next executed line in the entire program. You have to step out of code when you need to know the next line after the method selected.

How to do it...

In order to step through code, you just need to be in a debugging session. The rest is just a click away or just a matter of a keyboard shortcut. Perform the following steps:

1. Begin with stepping over the code. When your debug session is active, you need to press *F8* or select the button as shown in the following screenshot:

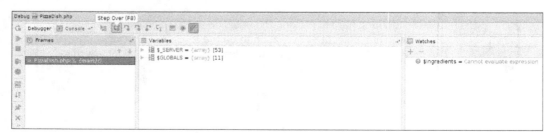

2. In order to step into the code, you just need to press *F7* or select the button as shown in the following screenshot:

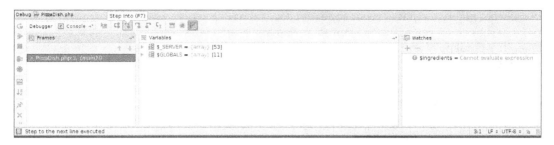

3. In order to step out of the code, you need to use the keyboard combination *Shift + F8* or select the button as shown in the following screenshot:

How it works...

Once you have used any of the stepping-through methods, you will obviously wish to know what goes on behind the scenes. A very high level of explanation will tell you that when you step into the code, the debugger takes you to the next line in the program. Once you are on the next line in the code, you can do a lot of inspection in that particular line of code, such as the contents of the variables.

Once you step into the code, the debugger actually shows you the immediate next line executed in the same program file or another program file. Once shown, you can again do lots of inspections in that particular line of code.

Once you step out of the code, the debugger shows you the immediate next line that will be executed after the current method is executed. If the debugger is unable to find any such line, the execution will be finished in the usual way, as it should have been without a debugger.

 You must have a debugging session before you try the shortcut keys such as *F8*, *F7*, and *Shift + F8*.

Running to a line of code selected

If you want no breakpoints in your code, but you still want the debugger to break at some point in your code, you are at the correct recipe and reading the correct text. This is also true when the breakpoint you set is already executed or stepped over, but you still suspect another line to be buggy.

How to do it...

1. To tell PhpStorm to ask the debugger to break at some arbitrary point of your choice, you should exercise the **Run to Caret** option. As a prerequisite, you have to place the cursor at some line of code in your program. Having done that, you have to now go to **Run | Run to Cursor**, and PhpStorm will obediently (and politely) ask Xdebug to pause at the location where your cursor has been placed. This is just the same behavior it would have exhibited in the case of a regular breakpoint.

2. There are three cases to be covered:

    ❑   One is when you have just started debugging your code; the execution will pause on the line you have specified.

    ❑   Another is when you specified a breakpoint in your code, and the debugger has proceeded ahead of that breakpoint (obviously after pausing there), the debugger will again stop at the line you specified.

    ❑   The third case is when you specify a line that will not be executed at all—if you have capsicum, you will not add tomato. In this case, the execution will continue past that line and move ahead to the next breakpoint or finish altogether.

```
$pizzaDish = new PizzaDish('New Pizza', 'Dish');
$ingredients = array(
    'salt',
    'cheese',
    ''
);

$ingredientCount = 0;
try {
    while ($ingredientCount < count($ingredients)) {
        if ($ingredients[$ingredientCount] == '') {
            throw new Exception("\nYou have run out of capsicum.");
        } else {
            $pizzaDish->add($ingredients[$ingredientCount]);
            echo "\nWaiting for capsicum topping...";
        }
```

Debug PizzaDish.php   Run to Cursor (Alt+F9)

Debugger   Console

Frames   Variables

                                          ▶ $pizzaDish = {PizzaDish} [2]
                                          ▶ $_SERVER = {array} [53]
PizzaDish.php:88, {main} 0

Run to the line where the caret is

How it works...

The working of the magic is quite simple to understand. Just as there were temporary breakpoints that disappeared once hit, this **Run to Caret** option functions in the same way. Thus, the line of code you place the cursor on becomes a temporary breakpoint, with the additional feature of being invisible. Thus, as soon as the breakpoint is hit once, it is automatically removed invisibly. If there is a line that will never be executed, the debugger simply ignores this location in the code and proceeds ahead.

 The keyboard shortcuts increase your speed. Use *Alt* + *F9* to be fast.

Watching expressions and variables

The most important utility of a debugger is that it actually provides you with X-Ray goggles with which you can see through opaque objects.

This phenomenon of *see-ing* through the opaque object (call it execution) is known as **watching**. It is synonymous with real-world watching. Do you watch something? You constantly pay attention to what is happening around that something to watch it. Daddy says, "I will see you son," and across the globe irrespective of the location, the problem of the son getting worried arises. But is the PhpStorm watching feature expected to worry you?

How to do it...

If you are determined to watch the whereabouts and howabouts of a variable, you can ask PhpStorm to do that for you. When you start debugging, in the debug window, there are three frames: **Frames**, **Variables**, and **Watches** open by default. To add variables to the watch feature, there are two methods:

- ▶ If that variable appears in the list of variables covered up to that point, you can select the variable, access the right-click context menu, select the **Add to Watch** option from the list. You will see that the watches section will have an added variable as this one.

- ▶ If that variable does not appear in the list of variables, you do not need to worry. If you remember the name of the variable you suspect, you can add it directly to the list of variables under watch (in the **Watches** window) by selecting the **+** sign and adding the exact name of the variable in the textbox that appears, as shown in the following screenshot:

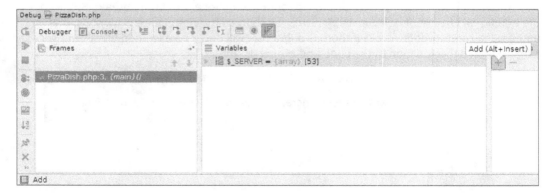

PhpStorm also enables you to add expressions under watch in just the same way as it does for a variable. All you need to do is to write an expression in just the same way as you would have written inside the editor. PhpStorm will take care of the rest.

How it works...

When a variable is put under watch, PhpStorm simply outputs the contents to the console, which happens to be a watch window. Thus, a variable put under watch is made to be visible at all times during the execution (debugging) of the program. If the variable value changes, the change is reflected immediately in the watch window. If the variable has gone out of scope during the execution, the content of the variable becomes **Cannot evaluate expression**. So it might appear to you that the content is not available, even though the content is actually available.

The same is true for an expression as well. The IDE treats it as normal content and attempts to show the value at all times. Just as it used to happen in the case of a normal variable under watch, the expression evaluates to **Cannot evaluate expression** if the expression contains a variable that is not covered in the current scope.

 Please do remember to use the *exact* name of the variable.

Changing code on the fly

According to no survey, it has been established that most of the bugs in programming arise due to uncertainty in the type and value of data. The real utility of a debugger is apparent when you have the freedom to interfere with the data that is generated during the execution. Thus, you can actually change the value of variables that the interpreter has covered while you are fighting against bugs in your code.

This can be particularly useful in cases where you have to set the width of a text container, and you cannot be sure about the maximum width of the text container.

How to do it...

1. The **Debug** view is your friend in this scenario. Focus on the `Variables` frame.

2. To assign a value to a variable, select it from the list of variables available.

3. Access the right-click context menu. Select the **Set Value** option, and in the textbox that appears, provide some value. You are done immediately after pressing the return key.

4. From now onwards, wherever this variable is accessed, it will assume this particular value. The keyboard shortcut to do this is provided by PhpStorm as *F2*.

How it works...

By now, you must have easily guessed that the debugger sits between your code and the interpreter. Thus, when you assign a value to a variable, the debugger *cheats* the interpreter by passing on the changed value as the original value. The interpreter, a poor blind creature, gets into this gotcha by assuming that the value is the one specified in the code and proceeds ahead using this value.

The world is not being trusted at all!

> When you assign some value to a variable, it is not that the value will be fixed irrespective of the business logic. As soon as a condition where the variable will change its value is met, the change will occur normally as it would have occurred in the absence of the debugger.

Code coverage in PhpStorm

Having set the platform to write clean code and to remove bugs from code to make good software, you must be thinking that your task is done, and you can now sit back and relax.

Not now! There's much more to do. Since you have promised that you will not tire and that you will not falter, you should have the fire burning within to proceed. This time, you are going to proceed with code coverage. Yes you read it right, code coverage.

This is the right time to get informed about this phenomenon now that you have working knowledge about a testing system (**PHPUnit**) and a debugging system (**Xdebug**). Code coverage is a phenomenon that is brought about by the combined functionality provided by PHPUnit and Xdebug. This means that you have to have both the systems installed on your development machine if you really want code coverage.

Getting ready

To solve matters such as these, there comes code coverage. No, no, don't think that code coverage will remove the unused lines—it will be *you* who will remove them. Coverage will let you know from where to remove the unused lines. Thus, code coverage is a phenomenon by which you check which lines of code are covered in the execution and which lines are not. Questions are firing inside you—what is the role of PhpStorm in this then? When you do code coverage, you get a visual indication as to which lines are not covered. It is this PhpStorm feature that takes care of managing this visual indication to you.

How to do it...

Covering a PHP code again requires some PHP code. You have to code everything in this world! The simplest way to code is to write tests for a target class. The framework (PHPUnit) will try to cover the entire class. In this case, you have to do nothing new while writing the code, for the change occurs when you try to run the test.

There is an option available in PhpStorm which lets you run a test with coverage. To do that, you will need to perform the following steps:

1. You need to select the test file and go to **Run | Run** <test> **with Coverage**, as shown in the following screenshot.

2. The target file will be tested in the usual way, and the coverage for the entire file will also be taken care of.

3. However, suppose you want to cover a selected part of the code or a method, you can do that too. There is an annotation provided in PHPUnit with the name covers. Using this annotation, you can tell the PHP interpreter that you want to cover only a selected part of the target class.

4. Thus, if you just want to test the getDishName method inside the (target) PizzaDish class, you can use something like the following code just before the testGetDishName method declaration in the PizzaDishTest class:

```
/**
 * @covers PizzaDish::getDishName
 */
public function testGetDishName(){
  $this->assertInternalType("string",
  $this->pizzaDish->getDishName());
}
```

5. There will be instances in your programming life when you will not want to do anything interesting. You will just bother testing code and not covering any code—you will just want to test. You have an option. There is an annotation available with the name coversNothing. This is a way to tell the PHPUnit framework "Ok mate, you will only do testing for me. Don't waste time in covering the code." Thus, you can write something like the following code:

```
/**
 * @coversNothing
 */
```

```
public function testGetInstance(){
  $this->assertInstanceOf('Dish', $this->pizzaDish-
>getInstance());
}
```

Having used the annotations, you successfully maneuvered the functioning of code coverage. Congratulations!

How it works...

The annotations are special features in PHP that provide some information to the interpreter to do some work silently. So, when you write @covers <Classname>::<Method-name>, you are telling the interpreter to cover certain code in a target class. Similarly, when you write @coversNothing, the interpreter understands that it does not have to do coverage.

Thus, PhpStorm provides you a visual indication by coloring regions in your code with certain colors denoting coverage and miss. When you run the test with coverage, there is a coverage view in the right-hand bottom corner of the editor window, which is shown in the following screenshot. You can view the statistics for the code that has just been tested (for coverage as well).

You get visual indications as well. It is shown in the editor window of the target class (here `PizzaDish.php`, as shown in the following screenshot) the area with red color is uncovered.

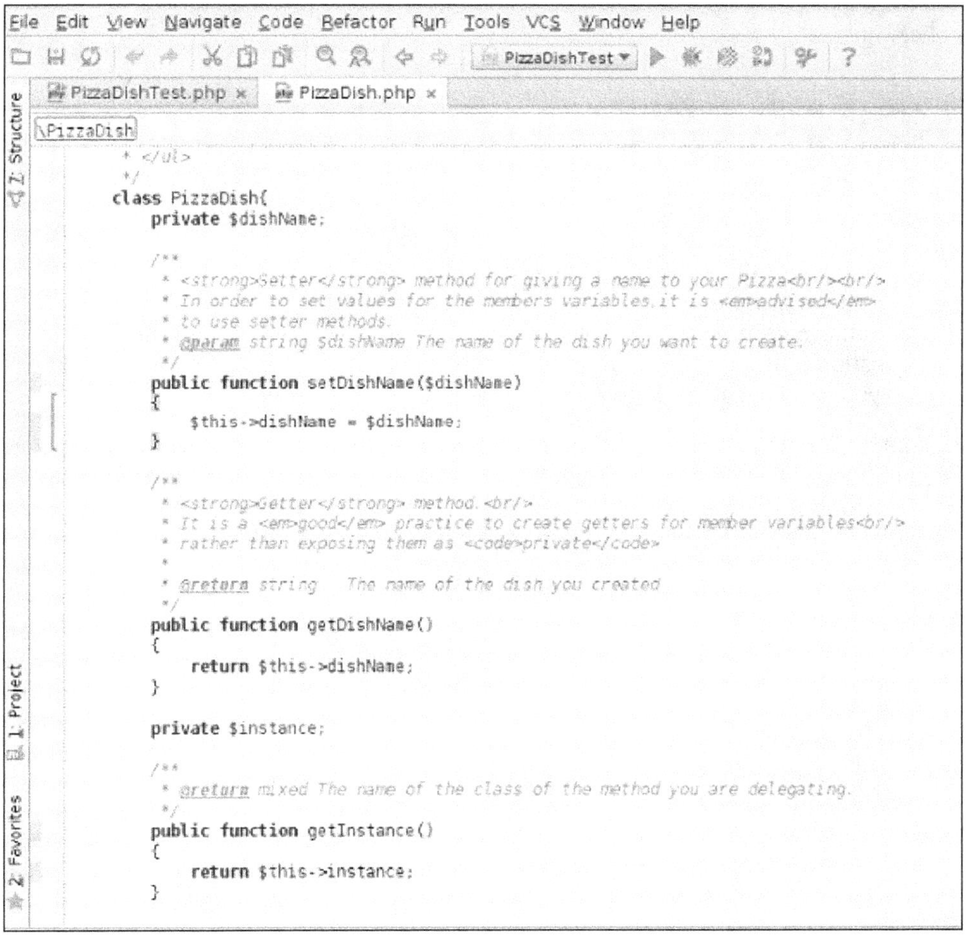

There's more...

Now we have learned code coverage in PhpStorm, it is time to see the purpose of code coverage.

Purpose of code coverage

Again, there's that same question in your mind: why do I need code coverage at all? The answer is not so obvious but is worth knowing about. You agreed that there were bugs in the code, so you used some debugging tool to find out and remove those bugs. You agreed that the algorithm you implemented went away at times, so you tested it and fixed it. But did you ever get a feeling that there might be unused lines in the code you have written? There might be lines that the interpreter will be unable to process, and there might be lines inside some conditions that are *never* met. Who will take into account these and many other such cases? Another question that will come to your mind is "what is the harm in having an extra line of code when you can have lines of comment in the code?" The answer is here.

A comment is something that the interpreter does not bother about, but an active but unused line is something that it bothers about. It is just like moving around in your kitchen with a pistol tied around your waist after you have come back from a shooting session. Would you need a pistol inside your kitchen? Why are you carrying it with you then?

6

Using PhpStorm in a Team

In this chapter, we will cover the following recipes:

- ▶ Getting a VCS server
- ▶ Creating a VCS repository
- ▶ Connecting PhpStorm to a VCS repository
- ▶ Storing a PhpStorm project in a VCS repository
- ▶ Committing files to the VCS repository
- ▶ Updating code from a VCS repository
- ▶ Synchronizing your code with the VCS repository
- ▶ Examining the VCS repository
- ▶ Checking projects out of a VCS repository
- ▶ Creating code patches
- ▶ Creating VCS tags or branches
- ▶ Creating a task for the team

Introduction

Rome wasn't built in a day. Nor by a single person...

Whichever sport you play or wherever you go, it has always been a team game. They have always kept on saying that united you stand and divided you fall. A PhpStorm cookbook author also used to say that reinventing the wheel is an action that should be avoided. Thus, you should always work in a team. The reason is obvious: a task divided among a team is completed faster.

According to a principle of software engineering, you should program in a team of two. This way, both of you will be able to discover errors in each other's code in the development phase itself.

So, when you work in a team, how will you work on an application development in which someone else is working on another module? One way is to use that same machine to code so that you can continue from the point where the other person stops working. But, is it wise to wait? It's OK that you work in a different shift. But, what if that person is geographically remote from you? Even if everything is favorable and if you need a third person to join the team, where will that person work? If you work for 8 hours, there can be a maximum of three people working on a project at any instant. Such inefficient usage of infrastructure!

How do you feel about the code repository? What do you think when someone says **version control** or **source control** before you? What do you know about VCS... VCS as in **version control system**?

What is meant by a version of software?

To get the answer, you have stepped into the world of version control systems. Welcome!

Getting a VCS server

The first action that you have to undertake is to decide which version of VCS you are going to use. There are a number of systems available, such as Git and Subversion (commonly known as SVN). It is free and open source software that you can download and install on your development server. There is another system named **concurrent versions system** (**CVS**). Both are meant to provide a code versioning service to you. SVN is newer and supposedly faster than CVS. Since SVN is the newer system and in order to provide information to you on the latest matters, this text will concentrate on the features of Subversion only.

Getting ready

So, finally that moment has arrived when you will start off working in a team by getting a VCS system for you and your team. The installation of SVN on the development system can be done in two ways: easy and difficult. The difficult step can be skipped without consideration because that is for the developers who want to contribute to the Subversion system. Since you are dealing with PhpStorm, you need to remember the easier way because you have a lot more to do.

How to do it...

The installation step is very easy. There is this **aptitude** utility available with Debian-based systems, and there is the Yum utility available with Red Hat-based systems. Perform the following steps:

1. You just need to issue the command `apt-get install subversion`. The operating system's package manager will do the remaining work for you. In a very short time, after flooding the command-line console with messages, you will have the Subversion system installed.

2. To check whether the installation was successful, you need to issue the command `whereis svn`. If there is a message, it means that you installed Subversion successfully.

 If you do not want to bear the load of installing Subversion on your development system, you can use commercial third-party servers. But that is more of a layman's approach to solving problems, and no PhpStorm cookbook author will recommend that you do that. You are a software engineer; you should not let go easily.

How it works...

When you install the version control system, you actually install a server that provides the version control service to a version control client. The subversion control service listens for incoming connections from remote clients on port number `3690` by default.

There's more...

If you want to install the older companion, CVS, you can do that in a similar way, as shown in the following steps:

1. You need to download the archive for the CVS server software.

2. You need to unpack it from the archive using your favorite unpacking software.

3. You can move it to another convenient location since you will not need to disturb this folder in the future.

4. You then need to move into the directory, and there will start your compilation process. You need to do `#. /configure` to create the make targets. Having made the target, you need to enter `#make install` to complete the installation procedure.

Due to it being older software, you might have to compile from the source code as the only alternative.

Creating a VCS repository

More often than not, a PHP programmer is expected to know some system concepts because it is often required to change settings for the PHP interpreter. The changes could be in the form of, say, changing the execution time or adding/removing modules, and so on. In order to start working in a team, you are going to get your hands dirty with system actions.

Getting ready

You will have to create a new repository on the development server so that PhpStorm can act as a client and get connected. Here, it is important to note the difference between an SVN client and an SVN server—an SVN client can be any of these: a standalone client or an embedded client such as an IDE. The SVN server, on the other hand, is a single item. It is a continuously running process on a server of your choice.

How to do it...

You need to be careful while performing this activity as a single mistake can ruin your efforts. Perform the following steps:

1. There is a command `svnadmin` that you need to know. Using this command, you can create a new directory on the server that will contain the code base in it. Again, you should be careful when selecting a directory on the server as it will appear in your SVN URL for the rest part of your life. The command should be executed as:

   ```
   svnadmin create /path/to/your/repo/
   ```

2. Having created a new repository on the server, you need to make certain settings for the server. This is just a normal phenomenon because every server requires a configuration.

3. The SVN server configuration is located under `/path/to/your/repo/conf/` with the name `svnserve.conf`. Inside the file, you need to make three changes. You need to add these lines at the bottom of the file:

   ```
   anon-access = none
   auth-access = write
   password-db = passwd
   ```

There has to be a password file to authorize a list of users who will be allowed to use the repository. The password file in this case will be named `passwd` (the default filename). The contents in the file will be a number of lines, each containing a username and the corresponding password in the form of `username = password`.

Since these files are scanned by the server according to a particular algorithm, you don't have the freedom to leave deliberate spaces in the file—there will be error messages displayed in those cases.

Having made the appropriate settings, you can now make the SVN service run so that an SVN client can access it.

You need to issue the command `svnserve -d` to do that.

 It is always good practice to keep checking whether what you do is correct. To validate proper installation, you need to issue the command `svn ls svn://user@host/path/to/subversion/repo/`.

The output will be as shown in the following screenshot:

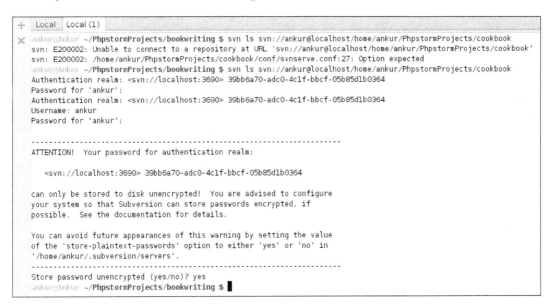

How it works...

The `svnadmin` command is used to perform admin tasks on the Subversion server. The `create` option creates a new folder on the server that acts as the repository for access from Subversion clients.

The configuration file is created by default at the time of server installation. The contents that are added to the file are actually the configuration directives that control the behavior of the Subversion server. Thus, the settings mentioned prevent anonymous access and restrict the write operations to certain users whose access details are mentioned in a file.

The command `svnserve` is again a command that needs to be run on the server side and which starts the instance of the server. The `-d` switch mentions that the server should be run as a daemon (system process). This also means that your server will continue running until you manually stop it or the entire system goes down.

Again, you can skip this section if you have opted for a third-party version control service provider.

Connecting PhpStorm to a VCS repository

The real utility of software is when you use it. So, having installed the version control system, you need to be prepared to use it.

Getting ready

With SVN being client-server software, having installed the server, you now need a client. Again, you will have difficulty searching for a good SVN client. Don't worry; the client has been factory-provided to you inside PhpStorm. The PhpStorm SVN client provides you with features that accelerate your development task by providing you detailed information about the changes made to the code. So, go ahead and connect PhpStorm to the Subversion repository you created.

How to do it...

In order to connect PhpStorm to the Subversion repository, you need to activate the Subversion view.

It is available at **View | Tool Windows | Svn Repositories**. Perform the following steps to activate the Subversion view:

1. Having activated the Subversion view, you now need to add the repository location to PhpStorm.

2. To do that, you need to use the **+** symbol in the top-left corner in the view you have opened, as shown in the following screenshot:

Upon selecting the **Add** option, there is a question asked by PhpStorm about the location of the repository. You need to provide the full location of the repository. Once you provide the location, you will be able to see the repository in the same Subversion view in which you have pressed the **Add** button.

Here, you should always keep in mind the correct protocol to use. This depends on the way you installed the Subversion system on the development machine.

If you used the default installation by installing from the installer utility (apt-get or aptitude), you need to specify svn://. If you have configured SVN to be accessible via SSH, you need to specify svn+ssh://. If you have explicitly configured SVN to be used with the Apache web server, you need to specify http://. If you configured SVN with Apache over the secure protocol, you need to specify https://.

Storing a PhpStorm project in a VCS repository

Here comes the actual start of the teamwork. Even if you and your other team members have connected to the repository, what advantage does it serve? What is the purpose solved by merely connecting to the version control repository? Correct. The actual thing is the code that you work on. It is the code that earns you your bread.

Getting ready

You should now store a project in the Subversion repository so that the other team members can work and add more features to your code. It is time to add a project to version control. It is not that you need to start a new project from scratch to add to the repository. Any project, any work that you have done and you wish to have the team work on now can be added to the repository. Since the most relevant project in the current context is the cooking project, you can try adding that.

There you go.

How to do it...

In order to add a project to the repository, perform the following steps:

1. You need to use the menu item provided at **VCS | Import into version control | Share project (subversion)**. PhpStorm will ask you a question, as shown in the following screenshot:

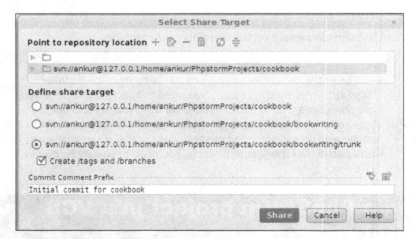

2. Select the correct hierarchy to define the share target—the correct location where your project will be saved.

3. If you wish to create the tags and branches in the code base, you need to select the checkbox for the same. It is good practice to provide comments to the commits that you make.

The reason behind this is apparent when you sit down to create a release document. It also makes the change more understandable for the other team members. PhpStorm then asks you the format you want the working copy to be in. This is related to the version of the version control software. You just need to smile and select the latest version number and proceed, as shown in the following screenshot:

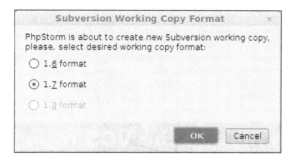

Having done that, PhpStorm will now ask you to enter your credentials.

You need to enter the same credentials that you saved in the configuration file (see the *Creating a VCS repository* recipe) or the credentials that your service provider gave you. You can ask PhpStorm to save the credentials for you, as shown in the following screenshot:

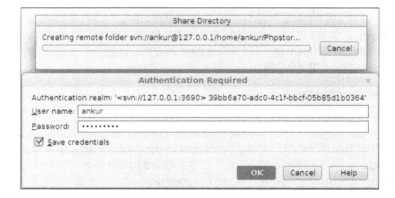

How it works...

Here it is worth understanding what is going on behind the curtains. When you do any Subversion related task in PhpStorm, there is an inbuilt SVN client that executes the commands for you. Thus, when you add a project to version control, the code is given a version number. This makes the version system remember the state of the code base. In other words, when you add the code base to version control, you add a checkpoint that you can revisit at any point in future for the time the code base is under the same version control system.

Interesting phenomenon, isn't it?

There's more...

If you have installed the version control software yourself and if you did not make the setting to store the password in encrypted text, PhpStorm will provide you a warning about it, as shown in the following screenshot:

Committing files to the VCS repository

Let's get back to a use case. By now, the memories of the Dish class must be under a thick layer of dust since it has not been used for a while now. Go ahead, mate. Remove the dust, shred the laziness, and set off looking at things from a different perspective.

Getting ready

A small amount of strain on your brain (and obviously reading documentation) will make you remember that you created the Dish class in a hurry. Now that you have matured enough to use PhpStorm as an IDE, you need to prove your might in programming as well. You need to make the Dish class more functional.

How to do it...

You can begin by peeping into the only method inside the Dish class. Once you do, you will clearly see that there is a FIXME tag. As stated in the FIXME tag, you should check for a valid ingredient name before allowing it to be added to the dish. This will prevent any unwanted ingredients from getting added to your dish and thus spoiling it. You need to specify two changes:

- ▶ You need to make the parameter default to a value in the method signature
- ▶ You need to check if the name is valid, that is, non-empty and not containing invalid elements

Thus the change you will make in the `Dish` class will be something like the following screenshot:

```php
class Dish
{
    /**
     * Add some ingredients to your dish.<br/>
     * You can do that by specifying the name of the ingredient.
     *
     * @param string $ingredientName The name of the ingredient to be added
     */
    public function add($ingredient = '')
    {
        if(strcmp($ingredient, '') == 0){
            echo "\nThe ingredient you have chosen cannot be added to your Dish..";
            return;
        }
        $ingredient = preg_replace('/[0-9]+/i', '', $ingredient);
        echo "\nYou have added: ", $ingredient;
    }

    //    TODO Add some method to check if the pizza is cooked
    //    TODO for ALice Please add the appropriate usecase for the checking functionality
}
```

How it works...

One of the main utilities of using an IDE such as PhpStorm is that the objects are shown in such a way that you get more information out of them. When you make the changes, PhpStorm starts indicating to you the changes using colors. If you add a line, it is shown in green, and when you delete a line, it is indicated by a gray triangle pointing to your right-hand side. When you make changes to a line of code, it is shown in blue. Besides this, when you commit your code, the version control number attaches another piece of information with it, which is quite important in itself. The information contains the user who committed the date, the time of the commit, and the revision number. The revision number denotes information as to how many times that particular file has been changed.

There's more...

PhpStorm, being a careful system, provides you with a number of options to choose from. You can tell PhpStorm to automatically update the code/directory after you commit if you enable **Auto-update after commit**.

If you want to keep the files locked during the commit process, you can enable this checkbox next to **Keep files locked**.

There are certain programming-related tasks before the commit action.

You can reformat the code you are about to commit by enabling the **Reformat Code** option.

You can remove unused imports/includes/requires from the code about to be committed by selecting the **Optimize Imports** option.

You can perform an analysis of the code you are about to commit by selecting the option **Perform Code Analysis**.

PhpStorm can warn you if you happen to push a TODO in your code to version control by enabling the **Check TODO** option. You can configure which TODO you want to view by clicking on **Configure**. Thus, before committing, PhpStorm will show you the TODOs you have created in the file/project you are about to commit.

You can even upload the committed files to an FTP server that you might have configured. Thus, PhpStorm can also deploy the code for you!

PhpStorm keeps informing you about all the files you have changed. The names of the files that have been changed locally since the last commit are shown in blue. The files that have not been changed are shown in black by default. If you are making changes to a file and another team member happens to make changes in the same file, there will be a text conflict, and such files are shown in red. However, such conflicts occur mostly during the update process.

 You can change the color scheme to one of your choice. For that, you need to go to **File** | **Settings** | **Editor** | **Colors & Fonts** | **Diff**.

Now that your changes are done, you need to commit the code so that it is made available to other team members. You need to access the right-click context menu, select **Subversion** | **Commit**. There is a dialog box that opens up and provides you with a view of what you are going to do. Once you are convinced that the changes are OK, you can proceed to commit the file. The file will again become black, indicating that it is in sync with the version control system.

 Avoid problems

It is not that you can commit and commit without problems. If another team member has committed in the same section of code in which you have made changes, the version control system prevents inconsistency in the code by providing you with a warning and disallowing you from committing the code. It throws a message that the file you are working is out of date. To avoid this problem from occurring, you always need to work on the most recent code base. Thus, always update before you commit.

Updating code from a VCS repository

You have always thought about your team. You have always thought that you will work in such a way that you are the strongest link in your team.

Getting ready

You will act as a filter to clean the poor code written by a fellow team member. You will be the peer reviewer of the code that your peers write. You will add documentation to the spaghetti code that someone in the team is so used to writing. All said and done, how will you achieve these targets? You will have to take updates from the version control system every time you plan to start off being the James Bond in your team.

How to do it...

Unfortunately, in order to receive updates from the version control system, there is no automatic push notification system provided with PhpStorm. However, you can perform the following steps:

1. You have to manually check for updates. But do not worry. You just need to remember a few navigation links, and you will be able to update a particular code, a particular folder, or the entire project.

2. The update link is available at **VCS | Subversion | Update file**. If you want to update the current file you are working on, use the option shown in the following screenshot:

Here, there are certain optional choices for you to make.

There can be a number of branches of development versions of the project you are working on. Suppose the management has made a provision for separate branches or versions of the project—probably one would be a new theme so that there can be testing, or there would be a separate branch to optimize the code, or any such permutation that is possible. Perform the following steps:

1. You can update to a specific branch of version control by selecting the **Update/Switch to a specific URL** option.

2. When you select this option, you can specify a branch. You can specify the URL as well.

3. This text box is populated by default with the Subversion path of the current file.

If you want to go back in time knowing that an algorithm used to exist in the past but has been removed now, PhpStorm provides you with an option for that as well. Perform the following steps to achieve that end:

1. You can select the **Update/switch to specific revision** checkbox.

2. There is a **Force update** option available to you that will force an update of the selected file.

When you enable the **Update administrative information only in changed subtrees** option, the PhpStorm SVN client will only update administrative information, such as the version number, previous revision, and file checksums-related versioning information for those files/ directories that have been affected by the update operation. Enabling this option might improve the performance of the update operation because there are fewer files to be updated, following the simple rule to do less in less time. Please note that under certain circumstances, you might have to perform a *normal* update.

 If you enable the **Ignore Externals** checkbox, the update will ignore all the external definitions from the update in the current file.

Similarly, you can update a directory that you select. In order to do that, perform the following steps:

1. You need to select the directory you wish to update, access the right-click context menu, and select **Subversion | Update**.

2. The same options will be available this time as well, but with the context changed to directory from file. Thus, when you force update, the *unversioned* changes inside the directory will be automatically added to version control, and the entire directory will be updated to match the repository copy.

 Since a project is also a directory, you can update an entire project as well. The method is exactly the same as that of updating a directory.

How it works...

The update action is quite simple to understand. Subversion (and other version control systems) maintains a working copy of the project. This working copy is created using a number of criteria, such as the date of modification, text that was changed, and version number. When you update the file/directory, all this and other necessary information is added to the working copy on your machine.

There's more...

If you wish to update your local copy with the copy under version control from the repository, there can be two possibilities, as follows:

- ▶ You are attempting to update a file/directory in which you have not made any changes. In this scenario, the update will happen normally.
- ▶ In the other possibility, if you are performing a normal update, there will be conflicts.

The version control system will tell you that it is getting confused as to which copy to keep under version control: yours or theirs? Select **Accept Theirs**, as in, the other team members, as shown in the following screenshot:

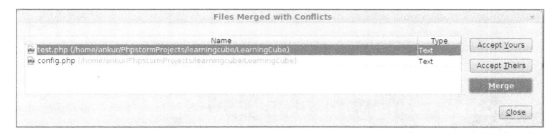

You need to calm down the version control system by merging the files and resolving conflicts. The conflicts are shown by PhpStorm in bright colors. Obviously, you can modify the colors as well. The red color is the conflict line, the blue color is the changed line, and the green color is the added line. You need to use the guiding arrows to send the content between the files, as shown in the following screenshot:

Synchronizing your code with the VCS repository

You cannot control where you were born. And you also cannot control which profession you choose: you just have to keep yourself up to date with the challenges the job presents to you.

Getting ready

One of the biggest challenges programmers face is to match up with the team. Due to a phobia of something unknown happening, programmers often end up in an unsynchronized version of the project on their development systems. They tend to follow Sir Isaac Newton's very first law of motion. The state of uniform motion is already described. The external force is the change in the business requirement and thus a new task assignment.

A short and simple solution to this problem is to always synchronize your code base with version control.

How to do it...

Code synchronization needs more care than any other action. The reason is obvious—you might end up accepting the incorrect version of the code and thus ending up asking for more time for development. You can synchronize the code in a number of ways, and the following steps help you with one of the ways:

1. You need to know the version control history as to which change was made.

2. You can do that when you select the project, access the right-click context menu, and select the **Subversion | Show History** option.

3. Select a version number that you want to synchronize your code base with. Access the right-click context menu and select the "**Show all affected files**" option.

4. You now need to select the **Show diff with local** option, and PhpStorm will show you the list of files in a hierarchical way, as shown in the preceding screenshot.

You need to select this button to see the list of files changed since your selected revision, as shown in the following screenshot:

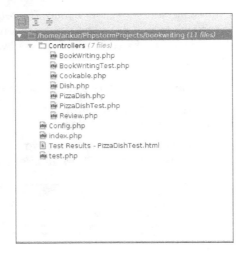

You can now proceed to view the individual differences in the file. You can select the changes you want to accept and skip the changes you don't want.

This can be a useful option if you know the effect well in advance, or else don't opt for this facility—it can prove to be annoying if the change list is large.

How it works...

When you synchronize, you are just performing an update operation—this time, manually and selectively. Thus, a synchronization process is copying the changes to your local working copy. The change can be anything: a new line of code written, removed, or changed.

Examining the VCS repository

The more you know, the more you know

More often than not, there are scenarios in which you need to see what is going on inside to be able to make decisions.

Getting ready

Having extra information always helps you to turn that last stone, which often proves decisive in the fate of a project. Thus, you might want to know what the structure of the code base is, what files are inside a particular directory, or even what directories are inside the project as a whole. Such wish-lists are endless.

Better work than just plan.

How to do it...

When you are determined enough that you will browse the repository, you can resort to PhpStorm. To start viewing what is going on inside, perform the following steps:

1. You need to select **VCS | Browse VCS Repository | Browse Subversion Repository**. Once you do that, you will be able to see all of the repositories you added while you were working with PhpStorm irrespective of the project, as shown in the following screenshot:

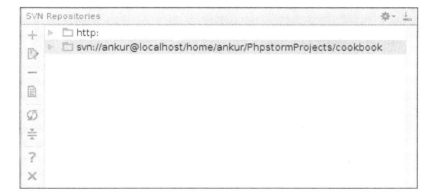

   You can select the desired repository location from the list of available locations.

2. Once you select a location, you can browse the repository by double-clicking on the selected entry. Besides this, you can do a lot more. There are a number of options available to you once you right-click and access the context menu.

3. You can create a new repository location if you select the **New | Repository Location**.

4. You can create a new folder in the selected repository if you select the **New | Remote Folder** option. You need to specify the name that the folder will be known by and a message to be displayed for this addition to the repository. Remember teamwork? Here's how **New | Remote Folder** looks:

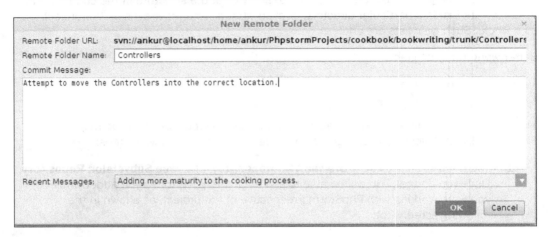

You can view the revision history for the selected repository location if you select the **Show History** option. Can you recall which other way you can view the Subversion history?

If you want to check out the project on your local machine, PhpStorm allows you to do that by providing you with an option with the name **Checkout**. This is similar to a hotel checkout, where you leave the hotel, taking all the luggage with you. Here, the analogy to a hotel is the Subversion server, and the luggage is the actual code. However, it is not a 100 percent analogy as you don't tend to check out someone else's luggage when you check out of a hotel room. Those are stunts performed by experienced professionals (pun intended). Don't try this at home (no pun intended).

When you are browsing, you might need to find out what is different in another code base version in a branched or tagged version; you have the option to do that using the **Compare with** option. Once selected, PhpStorm provides you with an information box that you can use to view information the way you like. You can select the version you want to compare with. It is important to note here that the order of comparison matters because you also have the option to do a reverse comparison. You can do that by enabling the **Reverse diff** option.

PhpStorm provides you with two options to choose from while obtaining the difference between files. You can provide a visual treat to your eyes if you select the **Graphical Compare** option, or else you can save the difference to a text file with the default name `diff.txt` in the current directory that contains your project.

You can search across the currently selected repository as well.

If you wish to search for the changes made by a particular author, you need to enable the **Author** option and provide the name of a valid author.

If you wish to search for changes made after a certain date, you can enable the **After** option and set the required date from a date-picker window available on clicking the button next to this option.

The same is the case when you want to search for changes made until a certain date. You need to enable the **Before** option. The date-picker window is available in the same way as in the previous case.

 If you remember the version number, you can browse the changes by revision number. You can select the changes with revision number greater than the **From** option and less than the **To** option.

How it works...

When you are done with specifying the search criteria, PhpStorm presents you with the list of changes that match your selected criteria.

PhpStorm says that you can do a lot more with this information and makes a provision for you to modify the search criteria, apply groupings on the basis of the date of change or the author of the change, and perform a regular expression-based search in this result. To see what options are available, you just need to right-click and access the context menu on the selected item. You will be provided with a number of self-explanatory options, such as **Refresh** to reload the search result; **Filter** to specify the search criteria again; **Show Details** to see the revision details quickly; **Create patch** to create a patch file of the differences in a selected revision; **Revert changes** to undo the changes made in the selected revision and to roll back the file/directory to the immediately previous state; and **Edit Revision comment** to modify the comment passed on to the version control system when making the selected revision.

Art is long and life is short, isn't it?

Checking projects out of a VCS repository

The phenomenon of checking out is quite interesting. You (usually) check out your luggage from a hotel room; you (most of the times) tell your friend: "Dude, check out my new Phablet"; you (are hesitant to) check out code from version control. What exactly does checking out mean? This seems more like a buzz word... checkout, checkout, and checkout!

Getting ready

Context is what you need to understand. The meaning of a word changes with a change in context. In the current context, you need to do what you are hesitant to do. Thus, checking out code is a phenomenon provided for version control systems, in which you take out the latest versions of the code base and download it onto your development computer. This download is not merely a simple download, it provides you with the latest version of code available under version control and makes you aware of the list of changes that have been made to the code base up until the current date. Thus, when you check out a piece of code, you become aware of the history of the code as well.

This time, before you get the answer in the *How to do it...* section, you need to know why you should do it. The team is what you were talking about when you started thinking version control. So, if a team has a new member, the only way to let the new member start working on the existing project is checkout. If your development machine has changed and you wish to resume working from where you left off, you can even use checkout for this.

How to do it...

To check out code from version control is everyone's cup of tea. Perform the following steps:

1. You can do it extremely easily by visiting the menu item **VCS | Checkout** from **Version Control | Subversion**.

2. Once you select that, you will be provided with a new window with the list of Subversion repositories you connected in PhpStorm irrespective of the project, as shown in the following screenshot:

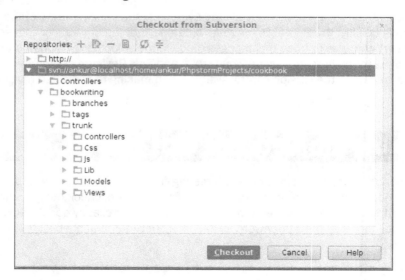

Having selected the appropriate version, on proceeding, PhpStorm asks you where it should keep the checked out code base. You need to specify that, as shown in the following screenshot:

When you set the target location, PhpStorm remains inquisitive. It will ask you general checkout options, such as the depth to which you want to check out the code, whether you want to check out the latest code or only until a revision, and whether you want to select the externals definition, as shown in the following screenshot:

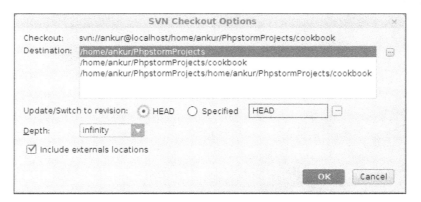

How it works...

Having set all the options, you can now easily sit back and enjoy the view. PhpStorm will check out the code and keep it in an organized way on your local (development) machine.

Creating code patches

It is often stated in three simple statements:

- ▸ Do it
- ▸ Do it right
- ▸ Do it right now

The statement is simple, but the intent is not. Every manager wants the task to be done, and it is you, the programmer's, headache to do it somehow. You often end up writing erroneous code. The misery does not end here; you happen to push it to Subversion at the end of the day to tell your manager what you worked on during the day. In this rush, you happened to push some bugs to version control. Thus, any fellow member working in another time zone will end up screwing his working copy by taking updates from version control. Now, there will be two types of resource wastage:

- ▸ That member (and any other member who's done the same) will spend time in locating the bug—a waste of person hours
- ▸ Having located the bug, you will have to undo the changes and make a few other changes—a waste of the previous person's day (when you pushed the buggy code)

Not only this, it will be an abuse of the version control system as when the bug entered version control, the very purpose of using version control was defeated—multiple people will be doing the same task—again, reinventing the wheel.

Getting ready

So, being the cause of this wastage, you must think of a solution to this problem. The solution will be to use an SVN patch. A patch is a file that is created when you create it. Obviously! SO, a patch, is a file that contains the differential text only and the details about the file where the changes were made. Thus, a patch can be applied to files and can be undone later. So, the code changes are visible only to the person to whom you have given this patch file. The advantage? The other person applying the patch can review the changes that you intend to make, and if some bugs are visible, the patch can be removed from the code base, and you can be informed that you need to do more work to create bug-free code.

You can view the applying of a patch file as an analogy to tailoring. When you happened to burn your shirt while cooking pizza (a business requirement has changed), you went to the tailor to get your shirt fixed (the business team comes to you to get the new functionality running). The tailor (you) finds a similar piece of cloth and shows you how by stitching it to cover the burnt part of your shirt (the code base). If you don't like the patchwork (the reviewer has found errors in the code), you can ask the tailor to remove the patch and try another color (the reviewer will ask you to make and implement another algorithm). The tailor easily rips off the patch and tries another color (you/reviewer remove/s the patch from the code base). This process goes on until you are satisfied with the patch (until the reviewer finds that your code is working fine). The tailor finally finishes the stitching properly and hands over the shirt to you (you commit the code and hand it over to the release engineer to proceed).

To sum up, you can create a code patch in PhpStorm.

How to do it...

If you want to create a Subversion patch in PhpStorm, perform the following steps:

1. You need to look up (in the top menu), find the menu item, **VCS**, click on it, and find the **Create Patch** option, and PhpStorm will show you a window that you might be familiar with.

2. Yes, it is a window similar to the **Commit** window, with the difference that the **Commit** button is replaced with a **Create Patch** button.

   And yes, the functionality is also different. You need to specify a comment that eventually acts as the name of the patch file (spaces replaced with a hyphen), as shown in the following screenshot:

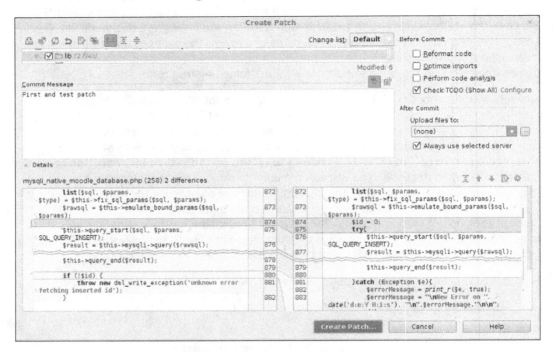

3. The default option is the easiest to understand and execute. Once you specify the (name and the) location where the patch information will be created, PhpStorm creates a patch right at that location, as shown in the following screenshot:

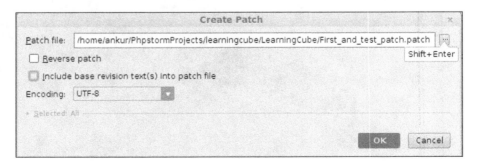

4. If you select the **Reverse patch** option, PhpStorm will reverse the comparison criteria—in the default case, it kept the latest version (**Head**) as the basis of comparison and considered the changes in this version as new.

5. While creating a reverse patch, PhpStorm will consider the immediately previous revision as the basis and consider the changes in this revision as new.

6. If you choose to **Select base revision text(s) into patch file**, it means you are asking PhpStorm to put in the contents of the file in the current revision. Thus, the file length of the patch file will be increased. Here, it is important to note that you can choose the file base revision you wish to include in the patch file.

Having made the necessary options and initiated the patch file creation process, PhpStorm will show you a success message along with an option to go to the location of the patch file now, as shown in the following screenshot:

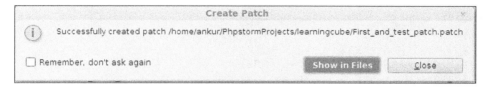

You can now pass on this patch file to the code reviewer, shut down your machine, and safely drive home without worrying about wasting any resources.

How it works...

When you create a patch file, you actually create a file that contains the difference between two files, or more precisely, revisions: the base revision and the would-be, next revision. So, a patch file contains the following information:

- the name of the file and the base revision
- the line numbers that have been modified
- the difference in the content

A typical patch file looks like the following:

```
--- lib/dml/mysqli_native_moodle_database.php (revision 258)
```

The changes are made to this file and the specified revision, as follows:

```
+++ lib/dml/mysqli_native_moodle_database.php (revision )
@@ -871,13 +871,20 @@
```

The line number changed is 871, 13 have been removed and, 20 have been added. Take a look at the following code:

```
list($sql, $params, $type) = $this->fix_sql_params($sql, $params);
$rawsql = $this->emulate_bound_params($sql, $params);
-
+ $id = 0;
+ try{
- $this->query_start($sql, $params, SQL_QUERY_INSERT);
- $result = $this->mysqli->query($rawsql);
- $id = @$this->mysqli->insert_id; // must be called before
query_end() which may insert log into db
- $this->query_end($result);
```

The - sign denotes that content has been removed. Take a look at the following code:

```
+ $this->query_start($sql, $params, SQL_QUERY_INSERT);
+ $result = $this->mysqli->query($rawsql);
+ $id = @$this->mysqli->insert_id; // must be called before
query_end() which may insert log into db
+ $this->query_end($result);
```

The + sign denotes that content has been added. Take a look at the following code:

```
- if (!$id) {
+ }catch (Exception $e){
+ $errorMessage = print_r($e, true);
+ $errorMessage = "\nNew Error on ". date('d:m:Y H:i:s').
"\n".$errorMessage."\n\n";
+ file_put_contents("/tmp/errorMessage", $errorMessage,
FILE_APPEND);
+ }
+
+ if (!$id || $id==0) {
throw new dml_write_exception('unknown error fetching inserted
id');
}
```

Happy patching.

Creating VCS tags or branches

The human brain is an overloaded machine. It tends to forget events or things or plans very easily. It requires continuous effort to make the brain remember things. Since a major part of the brain is dedicated to the visual sense, the most widespread usage to keep the brain on its toes is providing visual hints. Visual hints act in the same way as regular bookmarks would do in a PhpStorm cookbook they let you remember what section you were reading and when.

Getting ready

PhpStorm provides you with a feature wherein you can create visually appealing labels, that is, tags.

Tags are visual labels that let you and your team know which revision was special for you. Thus, you can create visually appealing labels or tags to denote special events, such as `Release Version 2.3` or `Bug fixes for V2.2`, and so on. So, where is the hint then? The hint is the name. Why visual? Because you can remember names and visuals easily.

How to do it...

The labeling process starts from the time that you decide to create a tag.

It should be a descriptive label because if you are not fully awake at the time of creating the label, you can end up with names such as `Tag 1` and `My Tag`. It leads to wastage of resources and abuse of technology as well. To create a tag, perform the following steps:

1. Anyway, if you want to create a new tag, you need to select the **Branch or Tag** option available when you select the **VCS | VCS Operations** pop up, as shown in the following screenshot:

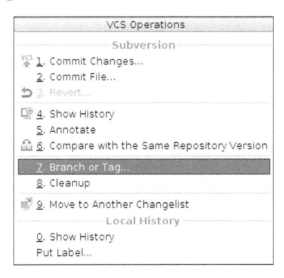

When you do so, you see PhpStorm asking questions in order to make you feel at home, as shown in the following screenshot:

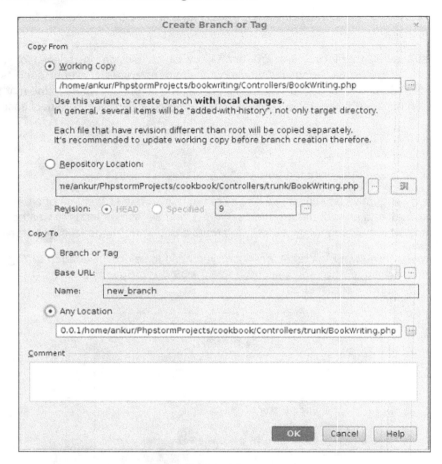

2. You need to specify the source on your development machine you wish to copy the file or folder from to label by enabling the **Working Copy** option and specifying the source file path.

3. If you need to specify a file or folder to copy from, you need to select the **Repository Location** option and specify the exact location in the current repository and the desired revision number or **Head** (the latest revision).

4. Then you need to specify the target where you will save the labeled version.

You can specify a location in the repository by specifying the base URL and the label name. This label name will be the visual hint for you.

 You can also specify an arbitrary location such as a repository location or even a location on your development machine.

How it works...

Once you are convinced that something works, it will be a great experience to go one step ahead and find out what goes on behind the curtains and what makes that thing work. So, the branch or tag creation process functions in the same way—when you create a tag or a branch in your repository, you just copy files from one location to another. Yes, it is the same copy that most of the engineers are experts at (no pun intended). Thus, there are four combinations available:

- ▸ You copy from your local working copy to your local working copy
- ▸ You copy from your local working copy to another location in the same repository
- ▸ You copy from another repository location to a location in your local working copy
- ▸ You copy from another repository location to another location in the same repository

 It is not mandatory, but it is always recommended that you add comments while doing anything—you can add descriptive comments so that you are able to relate this change to an action in the future.

There's more...

Having learned how to label a change in the repository, you can move deeper into the ocean of knowledge by proceeding to create branches. The similarity between a tag and a branch is that both are just folders with certain names. They are different in the purposes they serve. While a tag might be useful for small changes, a branch forms part of a bigger picture.

A use case will make the scenario clearer to you, and you will be able to differentiate between the two of them. Suppose the technology team has made a release, and they believe this is the last new development done for this version. So, you can make a tag named `Version 2.3 final`, add content to it, and leave it forever. Thus, at any time in the future, whenever you need to revisit your project, you will be able to recognize that "Version 2.3 final" meant such and such a release with such and such changes.

Creating a branch is similar to creating a tag since both are just repository directories. Perform the following steps:

1. To create a new branch, you need to go to the **Subversion** view, select the appropriate directory from the project view, and access the right-click context menu.

2. Select the **Subversion** menu item and select the **Branch or Tag** option. A familiar window will pop-up once you have done that. You need to fill in the basic information for the branch creation to proceed, such as:

   ❑ The source from where you access the files to be pushed into the Subversion: This source can be somewhere in your local development system (the file/folder you selected by default) or a repository location (you can specify the revision number as well).

   ❑ The destination where you will put the branch to be: This, again, needs to be a full pathname on your local development machine or a URL pointing to a repository location. It is important to note here that the repository location must be the same repository where your source resides.

   ❑ The comment you wish to add so you and the team remember the purpose of the branch creation.

So, you create a label to make a revision safe in the repository forever. You create a branch to make a safe and stable version of the code—a branch is created; you work on it, get it tested and approved, and merge it to the trunk.

> *It all is a matter of perception*

Creating a task for the team

Have you ever imagined how big things are created? How have people successfully managed to build large systems that function so well? What must have been their thinking and mindset when they decided to step out and attempt that extra mile?

The answer to this is quite simple. A journey of a thousand miles begins with a single step. So, when you started thinking about working with your team, you decided to work with version control. You went ahead and learned the tricks of the trade while working with version control. Now, it's the time for you to step out and try out that extra mile. Combine the knowledge you have gained, and get ready to explore one of the ways in which you can create a team task.

Getting ready

You want to create a team task so that you can set which section of code needs the attention of which programmer in your team. You can do that by combining the power of TODO (remember creating TODO tasks?) and version control. Thus, any fellow programmer will be able to know quite easily that such and such a task has now been assigned and there needs to be a proper development plan. A great help to the team—you will guide them through the correct way.

This also has a role to play in the peer code review process in the **eXtreme Programming** paradigm of software engineering, wherein you write code and your peer reviews your code. The peer then points out the probably buggy section in your code. Thus, once you push your code to version control with a task for your peer, the peer can push the changes they have made along with tasks for you to fix or consider or any changes that might appear as the need of the hour.

How to do it...

To create a task is not a difficult task (pun intended). So, if you want to point to another member in your team, perform the following steps:

1. You just need to continue your old style of programming but with a small modification: wherever you feel that more work needs to be done.

2. You just need to put a TODO followed by the description of the task you wish to bring to the attention of the team. The actual flow to create a general team task while reviewing code is as follows:

   - Find a piece of code
   - Have a thorough read
   - Write `// TODO <followed by the task to be done, for example, Add Documentation, team>`
   - Commit the code to version control

When you are writing code yourself, you can add a TODO to create a task to set the team thinking in a particular direction. The flow will be as follows:

- Write (refined) code—you cannot afford to make mistakes
- Find a logic that you think is not completely implemented
- Write `//TODO <followed by the task to be done, e.g. find some fool proof regular expression, team>`
- Commit the code to version control

When you want to divide the task among the team, you can use the TODO user followed by the name of the programmer you think would be the most apt choice in getting the work done. The flow becomes as follows:

- Read the changed code thoroughly.
- Test the code on your development system.
- Find possible improvements that can be made, and group them according to the caliber of the team members.
- Write TODO and the name of the target programmer, followed by the comment for each of the possible improvements that you found out. Some sample TODOs could be as follows:
  - `//TODO Alice`: This section needs to have the unnecessary variables removed
  - `//TODO Bob`: The actions inside a for-loop can be done outside the loop for lower execution time
- Commit the code to version control.

 This is just one of the ways—you are the person who will find out more and more ways of using version control.

How it works...

When you create a team task, you just create a TODO task and push it to version control. Thus, in a real sense, you are making use of the PhpStorm TODO feature. So, your TODO is actually passed on to the team members with the help of PhpStorm because it is the parser built with PhpStorm that recognizes the TODO keyword. Thus, when the team takes the update from version control, along with the other revision text, this TODO will also get included in your working copy. So, when a fellow programmer selects the TODO view, the intention is visible.

The same is the case when you create a TODO task for a particular programmer in your team. So, when everyone in the team takes updates from version control, the same TODO now contains the name of the programmer. This enables team members to focus on their task properly.

A team task not only helps the team to be more focused on the assigned task and put in more energy thereby, but also attempts to ease some pressure from the cumbersome task of allocating work to the team.

PhpStorm again to your rescue!

7

PhpStorm and Phing

In this chapter, we will cover the following topics:

- ▶ Connecting Phing and PhpStorm
- ▶ Catching Phing build file syntax problems
- ▶ Building a PhpStorm application using Phing
- ▶ Using a different build file
- ▶ Doing wonders with Phing
- ▶ Using the Phing build view

Introduction

Grandma used to say, "Don't copy, be original". Software engineering says, "Don't reinvent the wheel".

Whom do you trust? Trust software engineering if Grandma was not a software engineer!

They have copied and they have built great things that way. Saying "copying" could be controversial, so based on what is a more politically correct term to describe copying, let's go with *inspiration*. Thus, to state in diplomatic terms, they have got inspired from an existing software and created a new software altogether.

But, is this evil? What if that software did not exist? What if that software is quite useful?

Putting colors in this black-and-white picture, there was software: a build tool available for another language, Java, with the name Ant. People (the programmers) who were PHP enthusiasts thought of having a similar build tool, so some good people toiled hard and created **Phing** for the task. Thus, Phing has become a build tool for PHP, and it is said that Phing is Ant-based.

Some PHP programmers will say that when PHP gets interpreted, what is the need to have a separate tool for it? What is the use of creating a bundle when the PHP source code has to be given to the client? A simple directory containing the PHP scripts could suffice. The simplest and the most apt answer to this is that when you are a software engineer; you should always have everything automated—even the simplest of tasks as this one. Phing automates a number of processes: anything that you can imagine (in the PHP context). You can create an archive, check out code, deploy code, clean up logs, back up code—just think and there will be Phing (intentional rhyme).

When you work with Phing, you also need to understand what goes on under the hood. So, you write down instructions in the XML format based on some rules. These XML-based instructions are known as tasks for Phing. These tasks can be many, and the files that contain these tasks, again, can be many. It is worth noting here that you need to use proper (and documented) wisdom while separating tasks (or grouping tasks) because the more you stick to the principles of software engineering, the easier you will handle the compartmentalization better. Phing, in itself, is a code written in PHP (as already stated). This code, when executed, reads from the XML file you have written and obediently follows what has been written (provided the XML document itself is well formatted and adheres to the Phing XML rule). You can call this XML file the build file because that is its common name.

Did you notice that Phing has a strange name? It sounds more like an indicative sound of a commercial advertisement in between radio relay. Jokes apart, Phing is a recursive acronym—do you remember the first time you heard this word? Just remember that when you cannot remember anything, better start from the beginning (pun intended). Phing stands for **PH**ing **Is Not G**nu's make. God bless those who run so short on names.

Connecting Phing and PhpStorm

Having obtained some very basic information about Phing, now is the time for you to have some real-world action! Without PhpStorm, the action would have been centered on Phing, but since you are cooking with PhpStorm, you need to have a view from added angles. Thus, a probable roadmap for you would be to get Phing, install it locally on your development machine, and tell PhpStorm that Phing has been installed and that it needs to work in synchronization with Phing. Actually, PhpStorm makes use of the functionality that Phing provides.

Before we delve into the depths of building a build file, it is worth noting a few of the major features of Phing, which are as follows:

- Simple XML build files
- Rich set of provided tasks
- Easily extendable via PHP classes
- Platform-independent
- No required external dependencies

If you want to read more about Phing tasks, I recommend that you visit the official website of Phing (`http://www.phing.info/`).

How to do it...

To get Phing is everyone's cup of tea indeed. It can be downloaded as a phar using the command `wget -c http://www.phing.info/get/phing-latest.phar`. You can run this command in the terminal (which is accessible through *Alt + F12*). Once you do that, with a working Internet connection, you can have this phar downloaded. You need to note the path where the file has been loaded. It is recommended that you move the executables under a common folder that is not modified (doesn't have write permissions associated with it). It is not that there would be errors in it—doing that is good practice and keeps the operating system files and directories organized.

Having obtained the phar, it is time to tell PhpStorm about Phing. You need to perform the following steps:

1. Go to the **Project** view. Locate **External Libraries**.
2. Access the right-click context menu, and select the **Configure PHP include paths** option.
3. Provide the full path to the location where you downloaded (or moved) the package.

Bingo! You successfully told PhpStorm that you added a new library for the open project.

To make Phing available for all applications running PHP, you can add it to the PHP master include path—something like `/usr/share/php5`.

At this time, if you wish to check what changes were applied when you installed Phing, you won't be successful. You won't be able to see any Phing-related menu item anywhere in PhpStorm. You won't be able to see any extra icons, nor any extra views related to Phing. It would be natural for you to start considering that something was left out during the installation of Phing. Not to worry mate, stay tuned!

How it works...

To unleash the power of Phing, you need to execute it. To execute it, you need to have it installed. But you have already installed Phing, and you are not sure whether it got installed properly or not. This seems like a vicious circle. Phing needs an input file to understand what it has to do. This is known as the **build file**. So, you need to create a new build file inside your project. A build file is an XML document and is based on some rules. The default name is build.xml. So, a very basic build file looks somewhat like the following code:

```xml
<?xml version="1.0" encoding="UTF-8"?>
<project name="firstTask" default="firstTask">
<target name="firstTask">
<echo message="Testing Message 12...4"></echo>
</target>
</project>
```

Having done this, you need to do the following:

1. Open the Project view and select the build file.
2. Access the right-click context menu.
3. There will be a new option (magic!) available with the name **Add as Phing build file**. Select that option.

In order to check for successful integration, you can select **View** | **Tool windows**, and you will be able to see a new option available, **Phing Build**. If you can see this new option, congratulations, you have successfully connected Phing to PhpStorm.

> While creating a build file, PhpStorm needs to have at least one target specified. If you leave a build file empty, PhpStorm will be your friend in need.

There's more...

Since Phing is a software written in PHP, PhpStorm wants to have this software well within its reach. So, you add the include path to the project to achieve this target. When PhpStorm has Phing within reach, it attempts to create some options for Phing. For this purpose, it looks up to find out the build file and hence the targets. Once it finds the targets, it understands the targets and then creates the necessary options.

Catching Phing build file syntax problems

Now that you have worked hard to connect PhpStorm and Phing, you must know what drives Phing. What is it that allows you to do wonders with Phing? What is it that makes your life easier and makes adherence to the principles of software engineering easier? The name you had to think of was build file. Yes, it is the build file that controls the behavior of Phing. Yes, using build file, you can do wonders with Phing. Yes, using build file, you can perform tasks in a clean way—thus adhering to the principles of software engineering.

Getting ready

It's perfectly okay that you can write a new build file to perform tasks with Phing. But this question looms large—How do you check whether the build file you wrote is syntactically OK. Come on, if you say that you do not create mistakes while writing, you must be JARVIS and no human being. To err is human, to check and remove that error is *PhpStorm-ine*.

How to do it...

Before starting off writing build files, you need to know some very basic rules so that you can at least test a demonstration or Hello World actions in Phing. (Yes, you heard it right: it is possible to create a `Hello World` message using Phing.) A build file is valid to be used by Phing only when:

1. The file contains an opening and closing project tag. There should be only one, and it should be the root node of the XML tree. Inside the project tag, the file should contain at least one target tag: tags such as `property`, `tstamp`, and `propertyprompt`.

2. Now, revisiting the same build file, you will be able to understand the build file better—a second attempt makes you more mature as compared to the first attempt. Here, take a look at the following code:

   ```
   <?xml version="1.0" encoding="UTF-8"?>
   <project name="hello-world" default="firstTask">
   <target name="firstTask">
   <echo message="Testing Message 12...4"></echo>
   </target>
   </project>
   ```

3. In order to check the syntax, the inspection has to be taken care of. There is an icon provided in the bottom status bar. You need to click on it and set the **Power Save Mode** to off and the highlighting level to **Inspections**, as shown in the following screenshot:

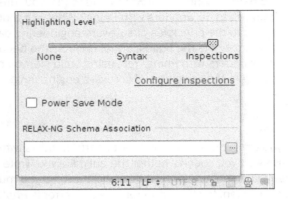

4. It is time for you to play around with the build file. Not to worry, there is the local history to save you—you can revert to some changes at will. So, whenever you make mistakes in the syntax, PhpStorm shows you errors:

   □ If you specify an incorrect start tag, a red underline will be shown in the nearest matching tags and the status bar shows a message **Start tag has wrong closing tag**.

   □ The wrong closing tag name will show a red underline in the incorrect tag and the nearest matching tag and the status bar at the bottom shows a message **Wrong closing tag name**.

   □ If you specify a tag that is not defined in the rule list of Phing, there are a number of ways in which the problem will be shown, such as the following screenshot:

❑ If you specify an attribute that is not defined or allowed for a tag, the incorrect attribute changes color to red, and the status bar shows the message **Attribute <incorrect-attribute> is not allowed here**.

❑ If you forget to specify the end tag for a tag, the status bar will show the message **Element <element-without-closing-tag> is not closed**.

PhpStorm at your disposal again, proves PhpStorm.

 Since you will often write tasks for Phing, you can also create a new template for the build file. To do that, you need to select the **File | New** option and select the **Edit file templates** option. In the window that appears, you need to add the name of this template (which will appear whenever you select **File | New**) and the extension of this template (you need to specify .xml) and put in the content of the most basic build file that you will always require. Clicking on **OK** will save this template.

The following screenshot shows a Phing file:

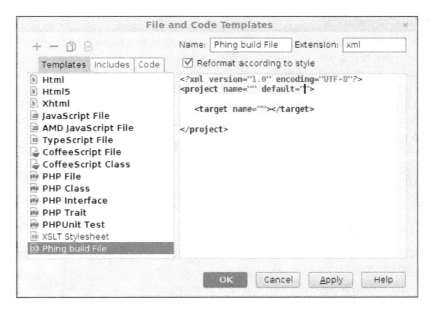

How it works...

PhpStorm inspects code on the fly. Thus, the general rules of inspection are applicable on the build file as well. This setting can be turned on or off by selecting **File | Settings | Inspection | Phing | Phing inspections**. So, as you keep on typing, the inspector keeps on checking what you write and continues showing you warnings visually.

There's more...

If you want to disable the inspections, you can do it in such a way that all inspections are turned off. Though not recommended, it can be handy in the case of large files.

Building a PhpStorm application using Phing

So, it is time for you to have some real-world action using Phing. It is time to give the problem of using Phing a shot (and get hurt by its shots as well). It is time for you to do something useful for the business of which you are the backbone. Fasten your helmet and set out to work in the sun.

The general meaning of build in other languages that require compilation is to compile the code, link the objects together, and create an executable. In PHP, though, you cannot compile the code; it is interpreted, dear: you can emulate the build process. How? Stay tuned.

Getting ready

To start with, you need to recall that you were hungry once! You must not forget certain things in life—one of them being your hunger. It makes you aware that you still need to work hard to earn bread to appease this hunger. So, when you were hungry, you just entered your kitchen and attempted to cook some pizza for yourself. Right? If you wish to pass on this same system that cooked pizza for you, what will your action be? You need to create a build file for Phing and write some targets and actions in it so that you are able to group together the necessary components and pass it on in one single unit.

How to do it...

To create a new build file, you need to perform the following steps:

1. Go to the **Project** view.
2. Select the appropriate directory, and select the build file type from the right-click context menu.
3. You will create a build file that will look something like the following code; don't worry about this code—you will get to know it in detail:

   ```
   <?xml version="1.0" encoding="UTF-8"?>
   <project name="pizzaCookingSystem" default="compressComponents">
   <target name="bundleComponents">
   <echo message="Creating a package directory." />
   <mkdir dir="./package" />
   <echo message="Making a list of components to bind together." />
   ```

```
<copy file="../Controllers/Dish.php" tofile="package/Dish.php" />
<copy file="../Controllers/PizzaDish.php" tofile="package/
PizzaDish.php" />
<copy file="../Controllers/PizzaDishTest.php" tofile="package/
PizzaDishTest.php" />
<echo message="Bundling process complete."></echo>
</target>

<target name="compressComponents" depends="bundleComponents">
<echo message="Compressing Contents of the bundled components." />
<zip destfile="package.zip">
<fileset dir="package" >
<include name="*" />
</fileset>
</zip>
</target>
</project>
```

How it works...

Finally, the time is ripe for you to understand the nuts and bolts that drive Phing. Thus, `<project name="pizzaCookingSystem" default="compressComponents">` creates a project element and binds it to a namespace with the `name` attribute. The `default` attribute defines the default target that Phing will select to execute. If you visualize the Phing build file in the form of a tree, a project is the root node of the tree. `<target name="bundleComponents">` creates a new target element that is a container for the actions that you want to perform. Thus, all the tasks that you wish to execute are written inside the target component. The target is selected by the `name` attribute. If you visualize the Phing build file in the form of a tree containing nodes and leaves, the target element is a node of the tree.

`<target name="compressComponents" depends="bundleComponents">` is another way of writing the target element with an added attribute `depends`. So when you specify the `depends` attribute, you specify to the Phing engine that this target element depends on some other target element. It is important here for you to be informed that when you specify the `depends` attribute, that target element is executed first as compared to the current element.

`<echo message="Creating a package directory." />` creates an element to echo a message to the console. What message will be displayed that depends on the contents of the message attribute. (Remember displaying `Hello World`? Your big smile is lovely!)

`<mkdir dir="./package" />` creates an element that creates a new directory in the current directory. This is synonymous to the `mkdir` command under `*nix` systems, which accepts the relative path as well as the absolute path as the target location.

```
<copy file="../Controllers/Dish.php" tofile="package/Dish.php" />
```
performs the file copy operation from the file location specified in the file attribute to the file location specified in the `tofile` attribute. This is synonymous to the `cp` command under *nix systems and accepts relative or absolute file pathnames.

`<zip destfile="package.zip">` creates an element to handle the compressing of files in the ZIP format. The `destfile` attribute specifies the name of the compressed file that will be the output. The output path can again be relative or absolute.

`<fileset dir="package" >` creates an element to set the files to be selected in the compressed output file. In other words, this picks up files from a directory specified by the `dir` attribute.

If you want to include selected files in the package, you can create an `include` element and specify the names of files you want to add to the output compressed file (`<include name="*" />`). Wildcard characters are acceptable here. Thus, a star (*) means that all the files specified inside the fileset element's `dir` attribute will be selected.

Now you can proudly say that you have the power to exploit Phing. Another feather in your cap, right? Excellent performance, keep it up!

Using a different build file

It happens frequently that you have mutually independent and exclusive tasks at hand. The principle of software engineering always advocates against grouping tasks together— modularity is the correct name of the phenomenon advocated. So is the case with you and Phing. What if you have a number of tasks to be undertaken? There are two routes to choose from: shorter and longer. The shorter way leads you to quick results but your friend, software engineering, will be offended. The longer way can irritate you at first, but dear friend, it would let you get more close to software engineering.

A wise decision is to befriend software engineering and take the longer route. Thus, you will create individual build files for individual tasks. Beware, though. Deciding the grouping of tasks in itself is a double-edged sword—it cuts both ways.

How to do it...

Having grouped the tasks according to their nature, you now need to concentrate on how Phing can come to your rescue in your overloaded daily life. You just need to follow the rules in order:

> ▶ **Group**: Grouping the tasks is an important step to begin with. You need to create a directory expected to contain the tasks (build files). It is not that there would be errors: this is good practice to follow. A person looking at your code hierarchy will be able to grasp your intent with ease in that case.

- ▶ **Create**: Creating the actual build file is the next step you not only need to do but also take extreme care of. Since this is the workhorse, you need to ensure that the program structure is minimal—redundant lines will confuse you. You need to write tasks according to the individual activities that you have grouped. Ensure that you don't leave the business team behind! So, to create the build file, select **File | New | Phing build file** option and write the tasks inside it. If you have not set any template for your build file, you need to select **File | New | File** and specify the name of the file with the extension `.xml`.

- ▶ **Setup**: Like always, your friend PhpStorm needs to be taken into account for your engineering needs. It is PhpStorm that makes your life easier—always remember. You therefore need to add the individual build files by selecting the **Add as Phing build file** option. This can be done by accessing the right-click context menu on the appropriate build file from the Project view.

- ▶ **Execute**: All is set now. When the need is felt, select the appropriate file and right-click to select **Run build file** option.

The following screenshot shows the build file:

Thus, PhpStorm did not let anything come between two friends—you and software engineering.

A sample build looks like the following code:

```
<project name="pizzaCookingSystem" default="compressComponents">

  <target name="bundleComponents">
  <echo message="Creating a package directory."/>
  <mkdir dir="./package"/>
  <echo message="Making a list of components to bind together."/>
  <copy file="../Controllers/Dish.php" tofile="package/Dish.php"/>
  <copy file="../Controllers/PizzaDish.php"
tofile="package/PizzaDish.php"/>
  <copy file="../Controllers/PizzaDishTest.php"
tofile="package/PizzaDishTest.php"/>
  <echo message="Bundling process complete."/>
  </target>

    <target name="compressComponents" depends="bundleComponents">
    <echo message="Compressing Contents of the bundled
components."/>
    <zip destfile="package.zip">
      <fileset dir="package" />
    </zip>
  </target>

</project>
```

How it works...

A build file is the only source to provide guidance to Phing. In other words, Phing only considers a build file fit enough to accept the execution requests. So, the different tasks are just a plural form of single tasks (no pun intended). So, the different tasks are written down in different build files, to ensure that the structural modularity is maintained. The individual tasks are executed depending on which task is required at any given time.

Doing wonders with Phing

What is art without practical usage? Practical usage means the utility of the art. The utility of the art clearly denotes the ability to solve a problem. So considering Phing as an art, it has got practical usage. Since it has practical usage, it has got utility. Since it has utility, it clearly denotes that it can solve problems for you.

What are you waiting for?

Think build problems, common or uncommon, think Phing. The most common problems are the most commonly known headache-causing agents—some of the developers in your team might not know the database specific language, some might not know the commands specific to the operating system, and some might not be trustworthy to be allowed to handle the system permissions; hence, the logfiles or temporary file cleaning tasks.

You can write Phing tasks to tackle them all.

Can you write a Phing task to check out files from the SVN server and deploy them on a target server? Yes, you can.

Getting ready

You need to have the **PHP SSH2** extension loaded. In `*nix` (Debian-based) environments, the PHP SSH2 extension is available with the name `libssh2-php`. It can be very easily downloaded with the command `apt-get install libssh2-php`.

You also need to have your SSH public key (most commonly a file with a `.pub` extension) added on the server on which you wish to deploy your code.

How to do it...

When you think Phing, you must be mentally prepared to handle the strict syntax of XML. So, you need to write some XML code based on the rules of Phing to:

1. Create a list of changes based on the Subversion revision number and save it in a file.

2. Export the changed files to your local server by reading from the file created in step 1.

3. Deploy the exported files to the server.

This is as simple as it seems. So, you would probably do something like the following:

```
<project name="SvnDeploy" default="prepareFilesForUpload">
<target name="svnLogin">
<property name="svnUrl" value="http://www.somerepositoryurl/
somerepopath"/>
<property name="svnUsername" value="you"/>
<property name="svnPassword" value="you@the-rep0s"/>
<property name="svnCodebaseName" value="name-of-code-base"/>
</target>

<target name="takeDiff" depends="svnLogin">
<propertyprompt promptText="Enter the starting revision number"
propertyName="startRev" defaultValue="1"/>
```

```xml
<propertyprompt promptText="Enter the ending revision number
(optional)" defaultValue="HEAD" propertyName="endRev" />
<exec command="svn diff ${svnUrl}@${startRev} ${svnUrl}@${endRev}
--summarize --xml" output="filelist.${startRev}.${endRev}" />
</target>
<target name="prepareFilesForUpload" depends="takeDiff">
<loadfile property="listOfFiles"
file="filelist.${startRev}.${endRev}" />
<property name="directoryName" value="uploads-${startRev}-
${endRev}" />
<mkdir dir="${directoryName}" />
<xmlproperty file="filelist.${startRev}.${endRev}"
collapseAttributes="true"/>
<foreach delimiter="," list="${diff.paths.path}" param="file"
target="exportFilesToLocal" />
</target>
<target name="exportFilesToLocal">
<php expression="str_replace('${svnUrl}/${svnCodebaseName}', '',
'${file}');" returnProperty="filePath" />
<if>
<not>
<equals arg1="${filePath}" arg2=""/>
</not>
<then>
<echo message="Exporting file: ${filePath} " />
<php expression="preg_replace('/([a-z0-9-_\.])+\.([a-z])+/i', '',
'${filePath}')" returnProperty="fileWithDir"/>
<echo message="Creating dir: ${fileWithDir} " />
<exec command="mkdir -p ${directoryName}/${fileWithDir}" />
<exec command="svn export ${file} ${directoryName}/${filePath} --
force" />
<phingcall target="deployFiles" />
</then>
</if>
</target>

<target name="deployFiles" depends="serverLogin">
<exec command="scp -r ${directoryName}/* ${serverUsername}@${serverUrl
}:${serverDeploymentPath}/"
checkreturn="true"/>
</target>

<target name="serverLogin">
<property name="serverUrl" value="localhost" />
<property name="serverUsername" value="ankur" />
```

```
<property name="serverDeploymentPath" value="/home/techie/Desktop/
deployment/" />
</target>

</project>
```

Heavy-duty XML code! You are encouraged to be brave enough to open the hood and see what goes on inside.

How it works...

Property Prompt is the Phing way to ask for user input during execution. The message that you want to show is to be written in the `promptText` attribute. The input value can later be accessed with the name specified in the `propertyName` attribute. If you want to set a default value to act as a fallback value just in case the user does not enter a value, you need to set the value of the default value attribute.

Exec is the Phing way to execute a command. If the command generates output that you want to use in another place in your code, you need to specify a name that will be the reference point to this output.

Phing enables you to load the contents of a file using this `loadfile` tag. You need to specify the path of the file (absolute or relative) in the file attribute. The reference name for this file is written inside the `property` attribute:

```
<foreach delimiter="A"list="${listOfFiles}"
param="file" target="exportFilesToLocal" />
```

You can iterate a certain condition using the `foreach` tag. The `delimiter` attribute separates the values of the input specified using the `list` attribute. The individual element in the loop is accessible using the value specified in the `param` attribute. The `target` attribute denotes which target is to be repeatedly performed inside the loop. Take a look at the following code:

```
<mkdir dir="${directoryName}" />
```

There's more...

Phing can create a new directory if you write the `mkdir` tag and specify the name of the directory to be created in the `dir` attribute. If the directory already exists, Phing remains silent and produces no message about the directory—you need to be careful yourself. You can call an arbitrary target in your build file using the `phingcall` tag and specifying the name of the target in the `target` attribute.

So, again Grandma was right. You created a larger and complicated object using small and simple objects. Always remember her values.

Using the Phing build view

PhpStorm is just. PhpStorm is good. PhpStorm does not discriminate. There are tool windows provided for every important tool provided to you. The same is true for Phing as well. So, you can have an overview of what Phing can do.

How to do it...

The Phing build view is accessible at **View | Tool windows | Phing build window**. The Phing view provides functions that are useful for Phing-related actions. So, you can:

- **Add a new build file to execute**: There might be Phing build files you have written in some other editor or obtained from another person. You can add those files as build files in PhpStorm. To add files, click on the **+** button.

- **Remove an existing build file**: If you feel that you have added an incorrect version of the build file, you can always recover from your mistake. You can remove a build file from the project by clicking on the **–** button. You can also use the *Delete* key on your keyboard.

- **Run a build file**: If you feel that all the targets have been written correctly, you can perform that action by executing a build file. To do that, you need to select a build file and click on the green **Run** button.

- **Apply target-hiding settings**: In the Phing view, you get a consolidated view of the individual build files and the targets you have written inside it. So, you can hide a target by selecting it, accessing the right-click context menu and clicking on **Mark to hide**. The hide settings are applied when you select this option available next to the **Run** button.

- **Expand all**: You can expand all the build files to show all the (unhidden) targets for individual build files. The keyboard shortcut to be used is *Ctrl* + (Numpad) +.

- **Collapse all**: You can collapse the build files to show only the build files and not the targets. The keyboard shortcut for the same is *Ctrl* + (Numpad) -.

- **Settings**: You can make settings for the execution of tasks by Phing. The settings window is accessible from inside the Phing view by the keyboard shortcut *Alt* + *Enter*. Inside the **Settings** window, you have the power to make a difference. Here's how you can do that:

  - You get a path to the Phing executable option wherein you can set the read or update the path to the Phing executable for the project.

❑ Then, there are command-line options that allow you to pass on certain options, such as `-l` (listing the targets) and `-debug` (setting the debug mode on).

❑ You can set **Properties** in the form of key-value pairs. PhpStorm gives you the option to select from a list of available macros or precooked placeholders. You can select which target(s) to hide or unhide by selecting or deselecting the **Hiding targets** checkbox.

Besides this, all other settings that are available to a view in PhpStorm are provided here. The options are: you can set the display mode for the view in one of the pinned, docked, floating, and split ways. You can move the window to one of the four regions (top, left, bottom, and right) on the screen; resize the window to a required size, hide the view altogether, and so on.

 The Phing application-specific settings that you create have to be created individually for each of the build files that have been added to PhpStorm.

How it works...

Here, it is important to understand how the Phing settings work. PhpStorm acts as a proxy for whatever tool it executes—it always creates wrapper (class) for the target tool. Thus, when you attempt to set the command-line options or add properties, you are telling this proxy application to remember that whenever the Phing command is issued, the arguments from the command-line options textbox are to be executed. In other words, you pass on the arguments to the PhpStorm proxy application, which in turn, executes the same old Phing command. The properties you set are used in the build file as is. So, when you set the properties, you are indeed making the properties persist till you yourself do not delete it.

8

Cooking Library Plugins

In this chapter, we will cover the following topics:

- ▶ Creating a library plugin
- ▶ Refining the plugin
- ▶ Configuring the plugin with PhpStorm
- ▶ Code hinting for the plugin

Introduction

Imagine a world where programmers such as you just enjoy writing code. That world seems enjoyable, perfect, and highly suitable for you in the first place. However, it isn't. What makes a programmer happier and satisfied more than anything in the world is the scenario in which the application reaches the end user. However, if programmers just enjoyed writing their code, who would ensure delivery of the code to the end user?

The end user can be anyone—a naive user, a professional user or even another programmer. So, regardless of the case, scenario, or end user, you, as a programmer, must be careful and concerned to make sure that whatever you code is (re)usable. Throughout your software-engineering life, you were told and you would be told not to reinvent the wheel. If you want this *dry* principle to be alive, you must make your code usable and reusable.

Another use case! Suppose you are asked to develop an application programming interface (API) in PHP. So, your task at hand is to write code. But another (untold) task for you is to ensure that the code you write can be included with minimum hassle. One quick solution to achieve this feat is to wrap up your application in an archive such that the archive itself can be included wherever required. Kindly read again! You need to have a bundle-like entity that you can pass on to the testing team to validate and verify. A wise programmer would advise the use of Phing to build the files together. However, the catch in this situation is that Phing will do what you ask it to do. However, do you actually know what to do?

You read it right that you need to create an archive. This time, we make use of a PHP archive, or phar, as they call it in the industry (`http://www.php.net/manual/en/book.phar.php`). Phar should not be alien to you. You must have used phar a number of times during your software engineering career. A PhpStorm cookbook author might have instructed you at some point in time as to how to get phar and include it in the PhpStorm library path. Can you recall how easy you used to find the task to have a PHP functionality in your project? If yes, it is the time to switch roles—from a phar user to a phar creator. If no, the time is ripe to learn how to create phars.

Phar is an archive file created in PHP. Like other archives, phars also contain a number of files and directories. To be able to use phar in your application code, you just need to include or require phar in your code. That's it! Phar would behave as if you included (or required) a regular PHP class. You will be able to use the classes, corresponding methods, and member variables that are declared inside phar (of course, the access specifiers will be respected).

However, having PhpStorm at your disposal helps you a lot. You can also include phar in the include path for the project so that a particular project is able to use the functionality provided by phar. If you need to make the PHP functionality available to all projects across your development machine, consider adding phar to the global include path.

PHP programming has always been fun. However, since you are an experienced member of your team, it is highly encouraged that you love your work while still taking care of the utility of the work.

Creating a library plugin

Have you ever thought about what makes up a library? A library is a collection of useful methods just as a book library is a collection of useful books. So is the case with an application library contains numerous useful methods and elements. The emphasis is on the word *useful* to stress the importance of not having redundant methods and elements in the library. A redundant piece of code requires documentation. When the company spends resources (essentially money), it will never want to have entities that have less usage. What is the reason for this? The principles of economics—the primary objective of any company is to maximize profit. No matter what!

Getting ready

However, not to worry, you do not need to be a Nobel Prize winner in Economics to stop putting redundant elements in the library. Just stay calm and stay wise. Cooking a plugin involves a number of engineering decisions to be made. Some of the decisions can be:

- **Decide what is that which makes you write a library**: You will not have the task of creating libraries too often. A library is a collection of a number of methods that you require a bit too often. So, to decide which methods are required, involves maturity.

- **Plan in advance**: Since a library is something that is used again and again without much modification, you will not get to release versions very often. Since the versions are released once in a while, if an incorrect plan creeps in while creating the library, it will be discovered very late that you do not have a big margin for error.

- **Make/reuse decision**: You have to decide whether the required library can be built by reusing another's or even your code that you created for another project in the past. Remember, you need to have a sharp memory for that. The other option to decide on is whether to create a library from scratch.

So, in essence, all the rules are to facilitate the creation of *phar* containing PHP code. Get ready for the ride!

How to do it...

1. Choose a directory containing the code you want to include for the plugin. Since you have been attempting to cook pizza, you can assume a use case where an end user needs an algorithm to cook pizza. There, you have the requirements!

2. Create a directory with the name `src`, which will contain the source PHP scripts. This will serve as the source for the library.

3. Create a directory with the name `build`, which will contain the target library, as shown in the following screenshot. This is the library you were longing for.

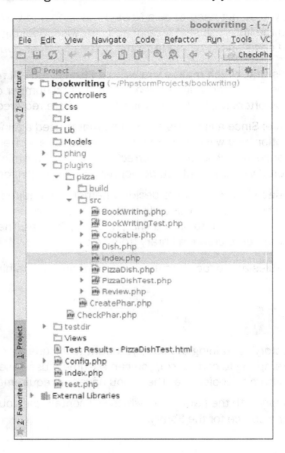

4. There is a change that you need to make inside the `php.ini` file. To find out which `php.ini` your system uses, you can type `php-ini` inside PhpStorm (do you remember the command window available by the keyboard shortcut *Ctrl + Shift + X*). You need to add the line `phar.readonly=0` to enable creating phars with PHP.

5. You will need to define an entry point for the library. What's the reason for this? This is the way phars behave. There has to be an `index.php` file by default. You need to put it at the top level in the `src` (or sources) directory. At the minimum, it needs to include a file that will provide access to the required class in the library (of course, you can change the name of `index.php` to another `file.php` and make it act as the entry point).

In the current scenario, you need to include the file `PizzaDish.php` so that you are able to cook pizza again—this time by the library. So, considering PHP code, you will write something like the following:

```php
<?php
require_once "PizzaDish.php";
?>
```

6. Since phar is a PHP functionality, you need to write code to create a phar package. You will write something like the following:

```php
<?php
$srcRoot = "src";
$buildRoot = "build";
$phar = new Phar ($buildRoot. "/pizza.phar",
FilesystemIterator::CURRENT_AS_FILEINFO | FilesystemIterator::KEY_
AS_FILENAME, "pizza.phar");
$phar->startBuffering ();
$phar->buildFromDirectory ($srcRoot);
$phar->stopBuffering ();
?>
```

With that done, you can sit back and feel happy having created a new plugin that you can easily pass on to the testing and the quality assurance teams.

How it works...

It's time for the nuts and bolts and grease and dirty workshop clothes!

You can see that you did nothing extraordinary: you just wrote very simple and native PHP code to generate an archive that will be available to be used as a plugin. You created directories to contain the source files and the build file(s) separately. This step was not a mandatory step, but it ensured that your working area remained clean.

The `index.php` file serves as the entry point for phar. Thus, when you include a functionality, you need to involve the reference to that functionality. This is what you do when you *include* `PizzaDish.php`:

```php
$phar = new Phar($buildRoot . "/pizza.phar",
FilesystemIterator::CURRENT_AS_FILEINFO |
FilesystemIterator::KEY_AS_FILENAME, "pizza.phar");
```

When you write this, you are initializing the phar-creating facility, which takes in the name of the expected plugin (the first argument), flags to pass to the parent class `RecursiveDirectoryIterator` (the second argument), and the name of the archive that will serve as its calling name. Thus, you will create a library that will have the filename `pizza.phar` and will be known as `pizza.phar` when you access it through the `phar://` stream.

You need to start buffering to initiate the process of creating the archive. Buffering is the process of writing to the disk until the time the buffering is stopped. It is done by `$phar->startBuffering();`.

The source files inside a directory are included in the plugin that you created when you write the following:

`$phar->buildFromDirectory($srcRoot);`

The process of including files to the archive continues until you stop the buffering of the output. You need to stop buffering to finish the process of writing the changes to disk. The archive that you wrote will not be visible until you stop buffering. This is done by `$phar->stopBuffering();`.

Once you stop the buffering of the output, the output (which was the archive file) will be displayed to you. How? In the form of the archive itself! Simple, isn't it?

Refining the plugin

Having a plugin by your side definitely encourages you. However, this encouragement can lead to some dire consequences if the software engineering principles are not applied to the plugin at hand. The plugin at hand can then lead you to become an engineer at bay!

Software engineering is the entity that does not let you forget it easily in whatever you do. You need to validate that the product you created (here, the plugin) is working correctly. Now, this *correctly* has a very broad meaning. Simply put, you just need to check that the plugin you created performs the intended action. Another aspect is verification. Having checked the intended actions, you need to check whether the action performed is correct or not. This is especially useful because the actual testing is done on the plugin according to this phenomenon.

How to do it...

You need to take two actions. Both are mandatory. The first is the validation part. You need to validate if the pizza-cooking plugin works or not. To do that, you need to:

1. Create a new PHP file.
2. Include (or require) the plugin you created in it.
3. Run this file, as shown in the following screenshot.

   If the run process gets completed as shown, it means your pizza is being cooked.

Now comes the verification part. You might need to verify that the dish you are cooking is actually pizza, else you might end up destroying your taste buds. To verify this is rather a vague sequence of steps, and it is not impossible to have different versions. The steps can be:

1. Check whether the classes in the plugin are accessible freely. You will need to create a new instance of the object. Thus, something like `$pizza = new PizzaDish('Mushroom', 'Dish')` should not produce an error. You should be able to use the object and the members in some external class in just the same way as you use a locally created class. Also, something like `echo $pizza->getDishName()` should not create an error about the unavailability of this function and should perform the intended activity correctly.

2. If a problem occurs in the plugin that you think is not in accordance with business requirements, you need to (obviously) fix it (quickly). So, you might need to again follow a few steps:

    1. In the `src` directory, locate the file (here `PizzaDish.php`).

    2. Identify the error-creating (or misbehaving) line(s).

    3. Make the appropriate changes.

    4. Create phar afresh with the changed source code. You might want to revisit the *Creating a library plugin* recipe.

3. Repeat steps 1-3 until the plugin starts behaving in the way it was expected to behave.

Whatever you do, you just need to have a refined version of the plugin.

How it works...

The working of the validation process is quite straightforward to understand. The validation of a product checks whether the plugin that you created is actually working as a plugin. Thus, you check for possible errors and problems in the process of using the plugin as a system. This is like saying, "Dude, check whether the plugin is working". Can you imagine who says this? A programmer says this to his fellow programmer!

The verification process needs to be understood. When you create a plugin, you don't know which agent will use it—it could be a command-line user, an IDE, or another bigger plugin. So, you need to ensure that the plugin you wrote is usable. Thus, when you create a new object, you check whether the classes that you intended to provide in the plugin are present. When you call a method, you check whether the method defined inside the plugin is accessible, and that too, no improper access specifier is restricting you from using the method.

The process of verification of the plugin is rather cyclic. Since it is your responsibility to ensure a proper functioning plugin, you need to repeat the verification steps until the quality assurance team is fully satisfied with the plugin. In the process, if you detect errors, you would have to go back to the source code to fix the problems and rebuild the entire plugin again.

So, the process continues for you. You write code. The code gets tested. You correct code. The code gets tested. The code gets tested. You create a plugin. The plugin gets tested. You go back to the correct code, and the process continues from that point. Cyclic, isn't it?

Configuring the plugin with PhpStorm

When it comes to saying that there is a plugin, it is to be assumed that there has to be a user of that plugin. Since you are a PhpStorm lover, you can safely assume that PhpStorm can be (one of the) possible users of the plugin. So, you need to act as a pseudo recipient of the library plugin and make an attempt to use the library. By configuring, it is to be understood as making the necessary adjustments in the project structure so that the library can be used to add functionality to the project. The age-old practice of reusability is at work, you see.

The main advantage that is associated with a library plugin is the ease of inclusion in a project. You just have to make use of this advantage.

How to do it...

To configure the plugin with PhpStorm, the steps to be followed are as follows:

1. Obtain phar from whichever source you wish.
2. Create a directory inside your project with a proper and descriptive name.

3. The plugin can be used very easily via `require(_once)` `'phar://name-of-phar.phar';`

All done! So simple—quite unlike what it appeared to be. This is the power of PHP unleashed.

There's more...

However, if you think that you want to do more with the library and are more interested in doing development by tinkering with the internal classes and/or packages, you might need to select certain classes in particular. This is done as `require_once 'phar://pizza.phar/Dish.php';`.

How it works...

The creation of a directory to hold the library plugin is not rocket science. It just facilitates obeying software engineering conventions. You as a developer or the plugin user is being referenced here. Thus, when you create a new directory, the code base of the project you are working on remains compartmentalised. So, when you need to change this library, you know where you have to go. Also, when you need to delete this library from your code base, you know where you have to go. If you are asked a question as to when you need to add a similar functioning library or some dependency, do you know where to go?

The way you use the library is dependent on the scenario. Recall that the library plugin contains two files: `PizzaDish.php` and `Dish.php`. If you want to use the basic functionality—cook pizza by adding some simple toppings and ingredients—requiring phar as a whole will serve the purpose. If you want selected functionality, specifying the name of the file relative to phar (inside phar) serves the purpose.

Since phar is said to behave in the same way as a PHP file does, when you included phar, the hinting also starts. Thus, when you write `phar://pizza.phar/` and press *Ctrl + Space*, there is a list of all the files contained inside phar shown to you. You can select one from the list in just the same way you used to do for regular PHP files.

Code hinting for the plugin

Here comes the actual utility of using an IDE for the plugin you created. It is a very common article of faith among developers that IDEs provide the autocompletion feature no matter what. However, at the same time, it is very uncommon amongst the same set of developers to know exactly how it is possible that the IDE provides autocompletion. Grandma always used to say *Ignorance never pays*. Exactly! Ignorance never pays (pun intended).

A question could be popping up in your mind. Why on the earth do you need to use the **autocomplete** feature? The answer to this might not be a diplomatic one, but it is true. In most cases, developers are ignorant enough not to write documentation for their code. Thus, autocompletion and / or code hinting serve as the saviors for the users of the code you provided. Since you are a programmer yourself, you can very easily understand the ease of using the code-hinting feature.

In the current context, you need to have similar settings so that PhpStorm is able to show you the documentation, method usage, and necessary information that is essential for a potential plugin user.

Getting ready

Enabling code hinting for a plugin is a one-liner. If you really want to configure code hinting for PhpStorm, you need to update the include path that PhpStorm respects. Updating the include path is done by opening the Project view and adding the location of phar to the list of libraries for the project.

How to do it...

The steps are as follows:

1. Select the Project view (*Alt + 1*).
2. Find the `External Libraries` directory.
3. Press *F4*.
4. Provide the location of the directory where you have the plugin located.
5. Click on **Apply** and press **OK**.

Done! Take a deep breath and press *Ctrl + Space* whenever you need code-hinting activation for this plugin. PhpStorm is again at your disposal!

How it works...

PhpStorm makes a lookup in the include paths that are available for the project and provides the list of classes and methods available in the current context. The system-wide include paths (`/usr/share/php`, `/usr/share/pear`, and so on.) are also looked up. Thus, when you add the phar to the include path, PhpStorm gets an additional path to look up.

So, the methods and classes available in phar (which you included in `index.php`) become available for code hinting. The code-hinting process covers the documentation, member methods, member variables, and every other thing that you designed to be available for use.

It is worth noting that when you add the library plugin to the include path, you start getting hints in just the same way as other methods available in the classes and libraries declared in the include path, but there is a difference to be noted. When you add the library location in the include path, PhpStorm is able to provide you with *only* the code hints. If you want to use the methods, you will not be able to do that. Another aspect is that when you need to use the plugin, and you `require (_once)` it, the code hinting is available then too, but this time *only* to the current script.

What is the difference, then? The difference is in the usage and availability of the plugin and its methods.

To sum it up, if you wish to use the plugin, you need to use `include (_once)` or `require (_once)`, and when you need the code hinting to be available across the project, you need to add the location of the plugin to the PhpStorm include path.

9
Code Quality Analysis

In this chapter, we will cover the following topics:

- ▸ Mess detector and PhpStorm
- ▸ Code sniffer and PhpStorm
- ▸ Locating code duplicates
- ▸ Code formatting and arrangement

Introduction

Engineering is beautiful. The beauty of engineering lies in the fact that it leaves no stone unturned and no path uncovered while carrying out even the simplest of tasks. Tasks that might appear too trivial for the lay person—even they are taken care of by engineering; software engineering, contextual.

You will agree that time matures you. Do you remember what your attitude used to be when you were a novice software engineer and when you were presented with a (programming) problem to solve? You started making plans using your infant knowledge about what the actual *code* would be like. So childish, right? As time progressed and you started gaining experience, you started using a scratchpad-like thing to first plan using primitive sketching techniques to visualize the flow of the algorithm. This was where you started feeling the need for engineering diagrams. You started learning UML—the mother of all modeling languages and the very basis of software engineering.

Time kept on taking you through the tough lessons of life. In due course, you realized that without following engineering principles, it was easy to start moving forward, but the way was one-sided and one-directional. Once you are required to go back and fix mistakes that you, as a human, have committed, the action can take you into a state of limbo where no one obeys the law of gravity. So, you and software engineering became friends, and life became much easier.

So far, so good.

If it is said that you can know a lot more about your close friend—software engineering—it is not incorrect or inappropriate. Software engineering not only helps you in maintaining ethics while designing a system but also keeps a track of the code you write. The number of lines of code you write, for example, can be one metric to determine the cost of software (considering that a line of code costs a fixed amount of money). The variable names in your code need to follow a strict standard. Why? It has to be a human being only who will be required to go through the code once some modification becomes the need of the hour. Since change is inevitable, the odds in favor of this event happening are high.

To sum it up, software engineering provides you with systems to perform analysis on this aspect of your software application as well. This process is known as **code quality assurance** since you are able to create code that is readable and hence maintainable. The systems available for you to achieve this milestone are known as **PHP Mess Detector** (**PHPMD**) and **PHP Code Sniffer** (**PHPCS**). PHPMD literally identifies and inspects the mess that a team member has done in the code base and provides warnings, error messages, and indications to not only clean up the messy code but also attempts to keep the code base clean. Code Sniffer acts as a sniffer dog and barks whenever it detects potential bugs in the code base. It is not that the combination of your eye and brain would be unable to detect simple errors in the code, but there are plural incidents in the development phase where you, as a tired software engineer, might commit very simple mistakes. With the passage of time, such mistakes grow to become a mysterious bug probably extremely hard to crack. PHPCS proves helpful in curbing such mistakes.

A question that is very obvious to ask: where is PhpStorm in the scene? The answer to this is that PhpStorm is always at your disposal. How? The two systems mentioned are used in conjunction with PhpStorm to wreak havoc on the bugs that attempt to creep into the development phase and keep on bugging you for long and sometimes extended periods of time. A waste of your bandwidth and thus decrease in morale—your manager will not let you go that easily till you are able to debug your application.

Mess detector and PhpStorm

PhpStorm is an obedient and diligent slave of yours. It ensures that none of your efforts get classified as scratchy or unengineered. How? It provides you with facilities to integrate systems, which in turn help you in letting your efforts achieve engineering maturity. You must be getting anxious as to which system is being talked about here. So, you can put your hands together for the mess detector known as PHPMD. A simple acronym, indeed. It is not that PhpStorm takes away all the due credit of removing the mess from your code, but yes, PhpStorm makes a provision for you to find out the appropriate version, download, integrate, and then start planning what to do. And then? Then what? Just sit back and let PhpStorm and mess detector collaborate and perform the tasks for you.

Getting ready

You need to have information about the latest (and stable) release of PHPMD. You can simply search it on the Internet via any popular search engine. The official website (`http://phpmd.org/`) provides you with information about the downloading methods available. Since you have a good taste for PHP archives, you can get phar from the URL `http://static.phpmd.org/php/1.4.1/phpmd.phar` (this was the latest phar available at the time of writing). Just like other archives, you need not take any other action—only this download will suffice with the executable.

When you talk about executables, since `*nix` systems treat all files that have been downloaded from external sources as read-only, it is your duty to check the access permissions on phar. In most cases, a downloaded file reads permissions only for the sake of security. You need to be wise enough to downgrade the permissions to allow appropriate access to this archive. On `*nix` systems, there is this command available, `chmod`, using which you can play around with the access permissions on a specified file or a folder. Thus (using `chmod`), you can probably set `766` as the permission string for this archive.

How to do it...

Now comes the important part—you need to tell PhpStorm about PHPMD. This is one configuration that you really need to ensure is in place. The reason for this being the beginning of PhpStorm is for PhpStorm to know that it has got a new member and thus needs to take the appropriate action accordingly. Perform the following steps:

1. You need to select **File | Settings | PHP | Mess Detector** and set the path of phar you just downloaded (or maybe borrowed from a friend), as shown in the following screenshot:

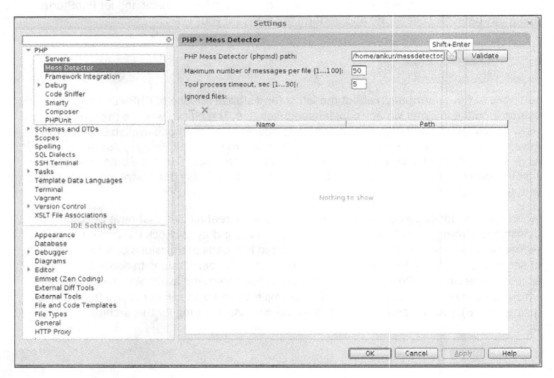

2. Validate the work you did. Don't worry. PhpStorm will help you as there is a provision to check for the configuration to be proper via the **Validate** button. If you have done everything correctly, you will get a green signal from PhpStorm, indicating the name of the software (**PHPMD**), its author, and the version number, as shown in the following screenshot:

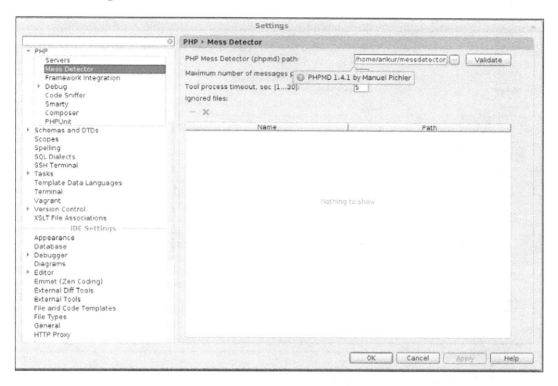

3. You need to configure the options available for PHPMD in PhpStorm. The settings are available at **File | Settings | Inspections**.

4. Turn on inspections.

5. Configure inspections by opening the settings wizards at **File | Settings | Inspections** and selecting the checkbox next to the **PHP Mess Detector** validation.

6. There is a certain predefined set of rules; you need to select some or all of them depending on your requirement. So, you can select one or all of the code-validation rules and proceed with writing the code. That is it. The following screenshot shows the **Inspections** page:

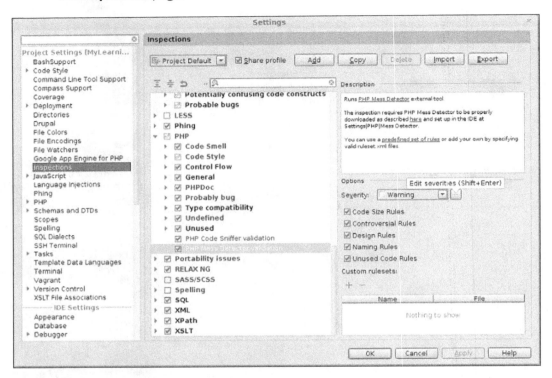

PHPMD will continue doing its work in the background and will keep on showing you errors and warnings as you keep on writing code. The notifications are classified according to the way you configured it.

7. To configure the notifications, you need to select the individual rule and make changes in the color, font, and so on, as required. The following screenshot shows how the Edit Settings\Colors & Fonts tab looks on the Severities Editor page:

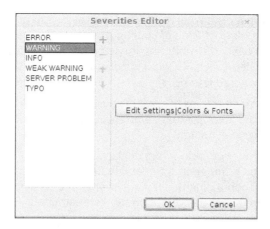

How it works...

Getting PHPMD to work is no difficult task. All you need to do is make a few settings and resume doing your favorite work—writing code. However, since you are an engineer, you should be keen to know exactly what goes on under the hood that keeps you going.

By default, PHPMD follows some rules. These rules were made while keeping in mind the principles of software engineering. There are rules to keep a check on:

- ▶ **Code size rules**: From time to time events occur which need you to keep a check on the size of the code. It is important to say that you write not only to write, but also to read it later and maintain it. One very important factor is the size of the code and the complexity associated with it.

- ▶ **Cyclomatic complexity**: Theoretically, a flow graph needs to be drawn to denote the algorithm in question, then the edges, the nodes, and the exit points are counted, and then the resulting number is obtained by edge count—node count plus the exit point count in the flow graph.

  PHPMD abstracts these details in its implementation. It takes into account the number of decision points, such as the loop constructs—if, for, while, case—and calculates the complexity as the number of decision points in the code plus 1 (one) for the entry point of the method.

- ▶ **Npath complexity**: Then, there is Npath complexity, which PHPMD takes care of. Npath is the number of possible outcomes in your code. It can be the cases under which the code produces output. So, PHPMD decides that a limit of 200 is OK for a code to be healthy. This means that your code (method) can have a maximum of 200 outcomes if your method is quality code.

- **Excessive method length rule**: PHPMD puts a restriction on the length of the method by counting the number of lines of code in it. This one is known as the excessive method length rule. So, if a method's lines of code count exceeds 100, that method violates this restriction, and PHPMD indicates to you in the form of a warning or whatever you configured it to be:

  - If the number of lines of code in your class exceeds 1,000, you need to refactor the class you have written. Who said this? The PHPMD excessive class length restriction.

  - If the number of parameters declared exceed 10, PHPMD will notify you to reduce the number of arguments to less than 10. You can then try passing an object containing the like arguments in one single object. This rule is known as the excessive parameter list restriction.

  - If there are too many public members inside a class, PHPMD treats it as bad quality and reports it to you via PhpStorm. The too-many factor is set to a default value of 45, exceeding which PHPMD starts treating your code as bad code.

  - Having too many private or protected members is not treated as good, either. If there are more than 15 such members, or fields, to be more technical, PHPMD notifies you. You need to restructure your class to have fewer fields. Why not try using composition? The *has-a* relationship... Remember?

  - If you have a little too many methods in a class that you wrote, beware. PHPMD will treat it as bad-quality code and will indicate that you need to refactor the class to have fewer methods in the class. The threshold is 10.

- **Controversial rules**: PHPMD treats code as bad-quality code when:

  - You have access to a *super global array* directly without encapsulating in some object.

  - You do not use the camel case to name classes, class members, and whatever variables you use in your code.

- **Design rules**: Code written in PHP will be a candidate for bad code when:

  - You have exit points in your code within regular code, such as exit points without exception / error handling lines.

  - You love using `eval` in your code.

  - You find using `goto` in your code enjoyable.

  - You have created a few too many children of a class. Fifteen is the threshold for PHPMD.

  - You have created a class hierarchy in which a class inherits more than six parent classes.

▶ **Naming rules**: PHPMD will also frown and thus indicate that the code is bad when:

    ❑ A variable name is too long or too short. A name is too long when it is greater than 20 characters in length and too short when it is less than three characters in length. Really short!

    ❑ A method name is too short to be understood. A name is too short when it is less than three characters in length.

    ❑ The constructor uses the name of the enclosing class.

    ❑ The constants in the class are written in lower case with words separated by an underscore (_).

▶ **Unused code rules**: Leaving the code unused is not looked upon by PHPMD with high regard. According to PHPMD, code is bad when:

    ❑ You have declared, and/or assigned a value to a local variable or a private field.

    ❑ You have declared and/or defined a method but have not used it.

    ❑ You have declared a formal parameter to a method but haven't used it.

Here is PHPMD in action. You can see how PHPMD provides errors and warnings as you keep on writing the code:

```
Too many messages per line...
phpmd: The method checkError() has a Cyclomatic Complexity of 10. The configured cyclomatic complexity threshold is 10.
phpmd: The parameter $date_expire is not named in camelCase.
phpmd: The parameter $date_start is not named in camelCase.
phpmd: The variable $date_start is not named in camelCase.
phpmd: checkError accesses the super-global variable $_COOKIE.
Missing PHPDoc comment more... (Ctrl+F1)
```

There's more...

If you are convinced that the predefined rulesets are not sufficient to support your cause, you can have your own version of the ruleset file added to PhpStorm. All you need to do is create a new XML file, name it reasonably, and ask PhpStorm to incorporate the file, as shown in the following screenshot:

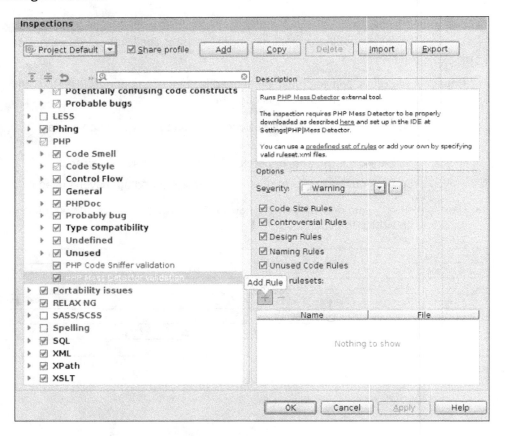

Your ruleset file looks somewhat like the following code:

```
<?xml version="1.0" encoding="UTF-8"?>
<ruleset name="test-ruleset"
xmlns="http://pmd.sf.net/ruleset/1.0.0"
xmlns:xsi="http://www.w3.org/2001/XMLSchema-instance"
xsi:schemaLocation="http://pmd.sf.net/ruleset/1.0.0 http://pmd.sf.net/
ruleset_xml_schema.xsd"
xsi:noNamespaceSchemaLocation="http://pmd.sf.net/ruleset_xml_schem
a.xsd">
```

```
<description>A custom ruleset - You can do wonders with this.
</description>
<rule ref="rulesets/codesize.xml/TooManyFields"/>
</ruleset>
```

The actual detection is done when you write `<rule ref="rulesets/codesize.xml/TooManyFields"/>` because it is this line that selects which option should be turned on for PHPMD. The other lines written at the beginning—you need not boggle your mind—just comprise the basic skeleton part. The best part of the story is that you need not remember the lines: you can just copy the lines from here and paste it to any `ruleset.xml` that you wish. The only thing you need to remember is the exact name of the rule that you wish to apply.

Code sniffer and PhpStorm

Have you noticed why defense personnel keep sniffer dogs? No? The purpose of the sniffer dogs is to sniff items around and detect for any illegal items present in those items. You might wonder how a dog decides which one is illegal and which one is legal, and even if it does that, how can it inform the humans about the validity of the item. A dog just knows how to bark: it barks at both times, happy or sad. Everything said and done, the question still remains. How does a dog know about an illegal object?

The answer is straight, abrupt, and terse: a dog is *configured* or trained to do that.

You have PhpStorm, right? You have been using it for all your programming needs, right? You can similarly use PhpStorm to sniff your code and inform you if the code contains some coding standard violation. The system that provides this functionality to PhpStorm is PHPCS or PHP Code Sniffer.

PHP Code Sniffer is a PHP5 script that tokenizes PHP, JavaScript, and CSS files to detect violations of a defined coding standard. It is an essential development tool that ensures that your code remains clean and consistent. It can also help prevent common semantic errors made by developers.

PHPCS is an application written in PHP that can be configured with a predefined or custom set of coding rules. It detects possible inconsistency and unclean code and thus does not allow common semantic errors to pass through in the production code.

Getting ready

Before you even plan to start code-sniffing, you need to download PHPCS as `.tgz` so that you have the installation file ready in your local system. The file can be downloaded from `http://download.pear.php.net/package/PHP_CodeSniffer-2.0.0a2.tgz`. After this, comes the installation. The PHPCS installation is quite simple in PhpStorm (just as easy as the other actions are). You need to perform the following steps:

1. Extract the contents of the tgz file you downloaded to a convenient location on your development machine—usually the computer where you play around with PhpStorm.

2. Inside the extracted directory, locate the `phpcs` file, which is a script written in PHP. This would most probably be inside the scripts directory.

3. Check whether the permissions set on the executable are sufficient to allow PhpStorm to use it. If you find something doubtful, set the permission to `755` on this PHPCS file.

4. Carry out the most important step. You need to tell PhpStorm that there is PHPCS available. For that, you need to select **File | Settings | Code Sniffer** and set the path to this PHPCS, as shown in the following screenshot:

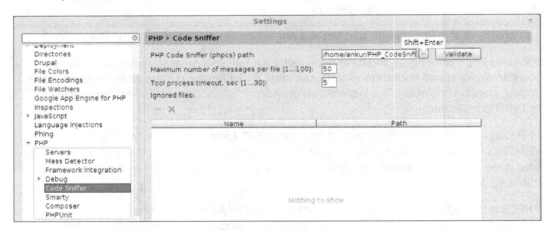

5. Validate that the settings have been made properly and that everything is OK in there, as shown in the following screenshot:

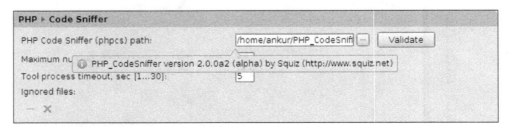

How to do it...

Having configured the code sniffer system with PhpStorm, you don't have to bother about how to make PHPCS work. It just works in the background with the default inspection system provided. However, you need to turn it on. The code sniffing process can be started by selecting the inspection option available for PHPCS:

1. In the bottom-right corner, there is this inspection icon available. You need to click on it and click on the **Configure inspection** option available, or the same option can be availed of by selecting **File | Settings | Inspections**.

2. You need to select the PHP inspection tree, and inside it, the **PHP Code Sniffer Validation** option has to be selected.

3. Next to the coding standard, there is a dropdown. You need to select one of the available values.

4. If you add more values to PHPCS, you need to refresh the list of available standards. The refresh is confirmed by a message, as shown in the following screenshot:

5. Having done that, you can now focus on writing business logic for the organization you work for. PHPCS will continue in the background and will keep on showing errors as you proceed. One of the errors is shown in the following screenshot:

```
        print_row(get_string('courseprofiles').':', rtrim($courselisting,','));
phpcs: [x] No space found after comma in function call
```

How it works...

The working of PHPCS is not very difficult to understand—especially for people such as you, who are (already) familiar with systems like PHPMD (it's another code quality assurance tool, just in case you were not familiar with it. Pun intended!). PHPCS also understands XML, and PHPCS also has inbuilt or precooked rules. This is clearly visible when you integrate PHPCS with PhpStorm. There are coding standards available to you via a dropdown containing these default values. This dropdown is available with the label **Coding Standard:** The PHPCS system obeys the standards and checks your code as you open it.

So far, so good. The actual nuts and bolts are located in the `ruleset.xml` file. No, no, it is not a typographical error as a result of engineered copy-pasting! The `ruleset.xml` file follows certain standards during creation. The rules that drive PHPCS are:

- Due to its being an XML, the most important line to be added is the XML version:

  ```
  <? Xml version="1.0"?>
  ```

- The parent node of all the nodes in the ruleset is the `ruleset` node. The name attribute makes the node known by a name to PhpStorm:

  ```
  <ruleset name="PHP Code Sniffer Standard">
  ```

- There can be a description node that contains the description of the standard under construction:

  ```
  <description>A custom coding standard</description>
  ```

- Then comes the actual rule. PHPCS can accept external references to a rule that someone else might have created:

  ```
  <rule ref="/path/to/some/persons/ruleset.xml"/>
  ```

- There can be a directory that contains code standards in the form of the PHP class hierarchy:

  ```
  <rule ref="/full/path/to/standard-classes/"/>
  ```

- Or, there might be a reference to a well-known coding standard, such as PEAR or Zend:

  ```
  <rule ref="PEAR"/>
  ```

- Some of the default standards are included as shown in the following code:

  ```
  <rule ref="Generic.Files.LineLength.TooLong">
  <message>Line longer than %s characters; contains %s
  characters</message>

  </rule>
  ```

Alternatively, it can have the following code too:

```
<rule ref="Generic.File.LineEndings">
  <properties>
    <property name="eolChar" value="\r\n"/>
  </properties>
</rule>
```

There's more...

Since the standards are defined in the form of the PHP class hierarchy, the inclusion also respects the hierarchical pattern in the `ref` attribute. So, the actual class that is referenced is the `Generic_Sniffs_Files_LineEndingsSniff` class defined inside the directory `/path/to/PHP_CodeSniffer/CodeSniffer/Standards/Generic/Sniffs/FilesLineEndingsSniff.php` under Version 2.0.0a2. The property being tried to be set in the class is the `eolChar`, which happens to be a public and string type member of the class.

You can find a sample ruleset file at `http://pear.php.net/manual/en/package.php.php-codesniffer.annotated-ruleset.php`.

Locating code duplicates

Business needs money, money needs engineering, engineering needs a plan, and the plan needs time. Since business needs money, and time is money, business does not want to waste time. Spending time means spending money, and all (software) businesses assume that money spent is money lost. Since business spends money sparingly, engineering resorts to code reuse. But then, the customer needs quality—after all, the customer has paid a (huge) sum of money to get the work done. This is a vicious circle.

When the engineering team is short of time, the challenge ahead is always to ensure that the copy-paste tasks are under control without side effects. Under control means that the software is able to do the expected work. The side effects are duplicate sections in the software, which can potentially lead to increases in the lines of code.

The situation seems grim!

You must remember PhpStorm at all times in your coding lifespan—whether you are having leisure or trouble. PhpStorm always has something or other for you. This time, PhpStorm will take you out of this vicious circle. There is a feature available that allows you to scan through your code and locate the duplicate code.

How to do it...

To effectively locate duplicates in the code, perform the following steps:

1. You need to select **Code | Locate Duplicates** from the main menu. You will get a pop up that is the selection-making point for you, as shown in the following screenshot:

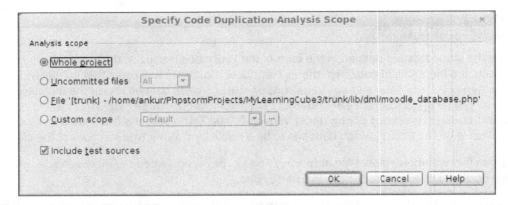

2. The default selection is **Whole project**. You have the option to find code duplicates in the whole project.

3. You can also set the criteria to work on the type or category of files according to the development cycle phase. You can choose **Uncommitted files** to locate duplicates in the code that you have not committed yet. This can be a good idea to improve code quality.

4. You can select the currently open file in the editor to work on locating the duplicate. PhpStorm also provides you with the option to set a custom scope of locating duplicates:

    ❑   **Project test files**: This is used when you want to locate the duplicate code fragments in the test files that you created for the project. This can be handy when you have a large number of test cases (PHPUnit test cases, to be precise).

    ❑   **Open files**: When you need to select the open files in the editor, PhpStorm will set the scope of duplicate search as the open files only.

    ❑   **Module**: When you want to analyze the non-project files, such as the libraries or the software development kits (SDKs), PhpStorm provides you with a facility by allowing this option.

- ❑ **Current file**: When you are quite sure that you want only the file that is currently open and is being actively viewed, PhpStorm provides you with this feature.

- ❑ **Selected files**: When you need to select a few files from the Project view, PhpStorm will set the scope of duplicate search as the selected files only.

- ❑ **Changed files**: Being an experienced professional, you might need to review the code written by fellow developers. This option comes in handy for files that are changed and are yet to be committed to the code repository.

- ❑ **Default**: This is used when you want to look for possible duplicates in the default change list for the changes to be put into the code repository.

 You can separately include or exclude the test sources for the duplicate analysis.

5. Code duplication analysis settings define the sensitivity of the search and set limitations that help avoid reporting about every similar code construct. The following screenshot shows the code duplicate analysis settings:

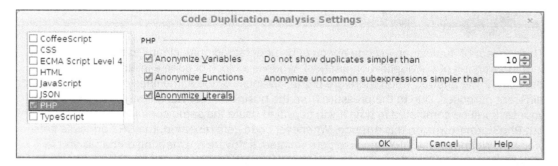

6. You can anonymize the functions, variables, and literals to save the memory heap.

7. PhpStorm can be told to limit the duplication analysis settings to dig only that block of code that is bigger than a particular size. The default size is 10.

How it works...

The answer to this question is honestly! Code duplication works honestly and finds out the duplications in code. So, after you invoke the duplicate code finder, it finds the occurrences in the file that have duplicate code. The duplicate code block is found out on the basis of the filtering that you specified in the settings (see the *How to do it...* section), as shown in the following screenshot:

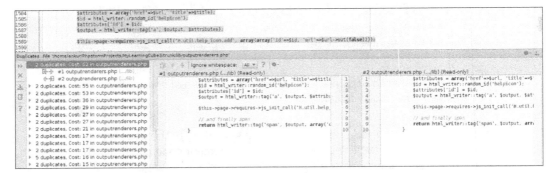

There's more...

The concept of duplication in code needs to be understood quite clearly to have an insight into the working of the duplication analysis. When is a block of code eligible to be termed as duplicate? The answer: when there are plural instances of the same lines of code rewritten for different purposes. Due to the pressure from the business end, you might get a feeling that your task will be completed in time if you copy and paste the same code for various tasks, but PhpStorm frowns on this attitude. Whenever code gets repeated, the *DRY* principle gets violated. Whenever the DRY principle gets violated, software engineering demands you to ensure code reusability. The most common way is to write classes and methods appropriately. Since PhpStorm is a great soldier fighting to keep the principles of software engineering upright, to ensure this cause, the duplication analysis lists all such occurrences in a dedicated code duplication window.

Code formatting and arrangement

A PhpStorm cookbook author says, "Merely writing code does not make you a software engineering warrior—an engineer becomes a Ninja when the code works and the person on the adjacent seat can make some sense out of it."

People might argue over this statement's validity. But since there is a general trend among engineers to develop dissatisfaction from their jobs, it becomes quite important for you, the senior software developer in the team, to have control over the way the code is written. Of course, it is your responsibility!

How to do it...

1. When you have got the determination to ensure that the written code has to be properly formatted, you need to select **Code | Reformat Code** from the main menu.

2. Like always, there will be a pop-up window for you to make selections. Quite happily, you can do wonders with this pop-up window, which is shown in the following screenshot:

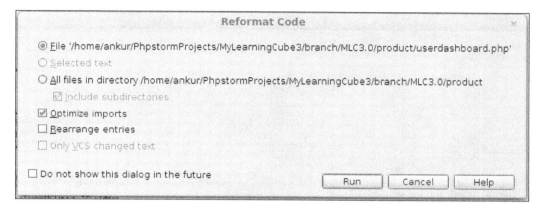

3. The default selection will format the currently selected file. Perform the following steps to obtain the required results:

   1. If you select text, PhpStorm will format the selected text only if the **Selected text** option is provided.

   2. You can select all files in a particular folder when you select all files in the **...** option. You can select the subdirectories inside the selected directory by selecting the checkbox adjacent to **Include subdirectories**.

   3. You can **Optimize imports** by removing the imports that are not required by the code.

   4. You can rearrange the import entries in the target code by selecting the **Rearrange entries** option. **Rearrange entries** will rearrange the order in which the elements in the code will appear.

   5. You can also reformat only the text that has been changed from Subversion by selecting **Only VCS changed text**.

   6. On selecting the **Run** button, the code formatting process does its work.

How it works...

The formatting system works by respecting the settings you have specified in **Code style | PHP**. You can control **Tabs and Indents** by selecting the tab, as shown in the following screenshot:

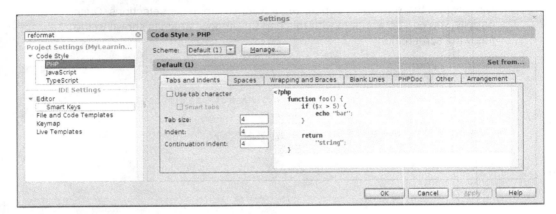

The spaces to be given in the code are controlled by the **Spaces** tab in the **Settings** panel, as shown in the following screenshot:

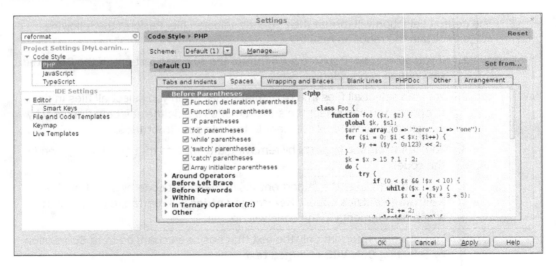

The wrappings and braces in the code are controlled by the **Wrapping and Braces** tab, as shown in the following screenshot. This tab specifies where the text will be wrapped in the code and where the braces will be formatted in the target code.

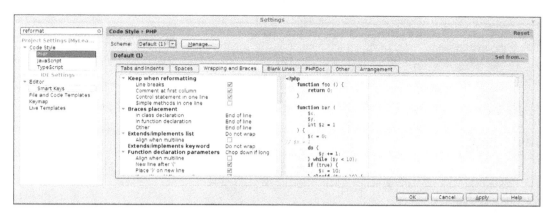

The blank lines are inserted at appropriate places in the code when the specifications are made in the **Blank Lines** tab, as shown in the following screenshot:

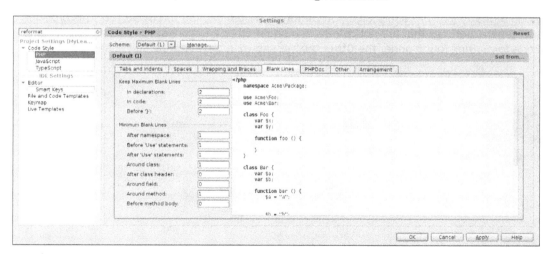

The PHPDoc can be formatted as well.. Remember this setting?

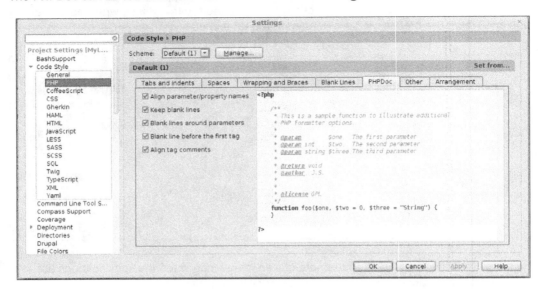

Code formatting involves miscellaneous settings available under the **Other** tab. This provides the general settings that are not categorized under other categories. The settings behind the code formatting found under the **Other** tab are shown in the following screenshot:

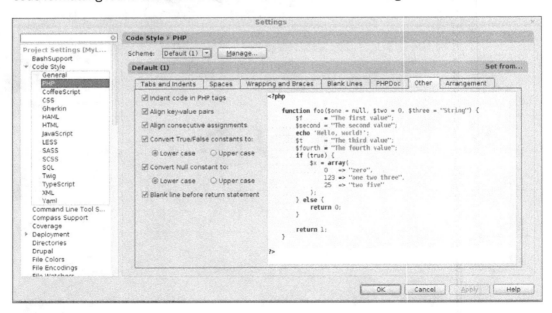

The arrangement of class members gets driven by the settings available under the **Arrangement** tab. The order in which the elements in the code are to be arranged is available under this tab. You can save the settings with the **Manage** button and can use it in other projects as well. If you already are in that "other" project, you need to select the text in blue **Set from...** to select the already-set formatting rule, as shown in the following screenshot:

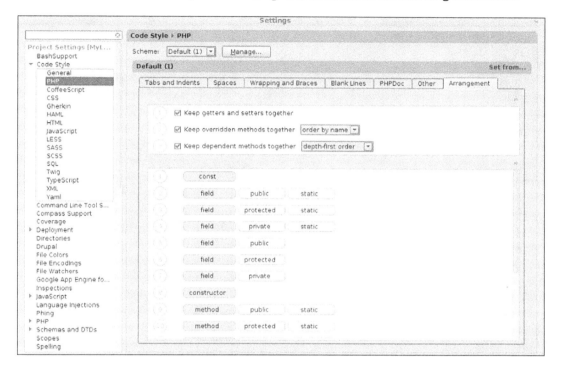

All done. Happy code formatting!

As a last word before leaving the kitchen, we, the authors, want to state that since knowledge is something that always keeps evolving, you, the (senior) software developer should not limit yourself to a limited set of knowledge resources. As an implementation of this rule, we plan to work on adding many more recipes that definitely were skipped due to deadline limitations. You can continue to follow the updates in the PhpStorm community; in the meantime, the authors will continue to work on PhpStorm to bring out more interesting and tasty dishes for you.

This is not the end, but the beginning of something more and something that is of the type *NeverBefore*. PhpStorm rocks!

Index

A

application
testing, with PHPUnit 124-126
aptitude utility 147
autocomplete feature 206

B

bookmark
creating 22
Toggle Bookmark option 22
Toggle Bookmark with Mnemonic option 23
braces 56
branches
creating 172-176
breakpoint
about 129
conditions, configuring 130, 131
permanent breakpoint 130
setting 130
temporary breakpoint 130
bug 120
build file
about 182
rules 188, 189
using 188-190
build file syntax problems, Phing
catching 183-185

C

class
about 42
copying 73
moving 74
renaming 70

class requisites, PhpStorm
directory 43
file extension 44
filename 43
kind 44
name 43
namespace 43
code
formatting 226-231
modifying 139, 140
running 92, 93
searching, in project 79-83
surrounding, with control structures 52-55
synchronizing, with VCS repository 160-162
updating, from VCS repository 157-160
code arrangement 226-231
code completion
using 32, 33
code coverage, PhpStorm
about 140-143
need for 144
code duplicates
locating 223-226
code hinting, plugin 205, 206
code patches
creating 168-172
code quality assurance 210
comment 144
comparison
used, for restoring elements 87
Composer
URL, for downloading 37
URL, for obtaining 37
used, for creating PHP project 36-41
concurrent versions system (CVS) 146
content root 31

controller
  creating, with Symfony 101-103
  creating, with Yii framework 109
  creating, with Zend framework 113, 114
control structures
  code, surrounding with 52-55
customization
  performing, PhpStorm used 26, 27

D

Database view 10
datatype 43
debugger 120
debugging 120
debugging session
  starting 127-129
debugging system (Xdebug) 140
delegate methods
  creating 50-52
delegation 50
deleted resources
  restoring 23-26
directory
  moving 74
  renaming 69
directory structure, Symfony
  app folder 99
  bin folder 100
  src folder 100
  vendor directory 100
  web folder 100
Don't Repeat Yourself (DRY) principle 73

E

editors
  maximizing 17
  views, linking to 20
elements
  copying 72, 73
  deleting 77, 78
  moving 73
  renaming 68-71
  restoring, comparison used 87
exception breakpoints
  about 132
  creating 132, 133

Exec 193
expressions
  watching 138, 139
eXtreme Programming 177

F

Favorites view 10
files
  committing, to VCS repository 154, 155
  comparing 84-87
files, custom scope of locating duplicates
  changed files 225
  current file 225
  default 225
  module 224
  open files 224
  project test files 224
  selected files 225
Find in path tool 79
first-decide-then-do principle 54
FIXME tags 65
functions, Phing build view 194

G

getter method
  adding 49, 50
GitHub 127

I

include path
  adding 29, 30
index
  unwanted directories, excluding from 30
installation, PHPUnit 120-122

J

JetBrains 8

K

key binding
  creating 21, 22
keymap shortcuts 21

L

library 198
library plugin
  creating 199-202

M

matching brace
  finding 56
member variables
  renaming 71
menu options, Database view
  Flatten Schemas 15
  Group Tables by Type 15
  Sort Columns 15
menu options, Favorites view
  Autoscroll from Source 13
  Autoscroll to Source 13
  Show Members 13
menu options, Project view
  Autoscroll from Source 13
  Autoscroll to Source 13
  Folders Always on To 13
  Select Next View 12
  Select Previous View 12
  Show List of Views 12
  Show Members 13
  Sort by Type 13
menu options, Structure view
  Show Constants 14
  Show Fields 14
  Show Inherited 14
  Show Toolbar 14
  Sort Alphabetically 14
  Sort by Visibility 14
menu options, TODO view
  Select Next Tab 12
  Select Previous Tab 12
  Show List of Tab 12
method
  moving 74
  renaming 70
method signature
  modifying 71
model
  creating, with Symfony 103-105
  creating, with Yii framework 107, 108
  creating, with Zend framework 111-113

O

object-oriented programming 50
Off-The-Shelf development 73
orientation modes, views
  Docked Mode 11
  Floating Mode 11
  Pinned Mode 11
  Split Mode 11

P

permanent breakpoint 130
Phing
  about 179
  build file syntax problems, catching 183-185
  connecting, with PhpStorm 180-182
  practical usage 190-193
  URL 181
  used, for building PhpStorm
      application 186-188
Phing build view
  functions 194
  using 194, 195
PHP Archive (PHAR) 121
PHP class
  creating 42-44
PHP Code Sniffer (PHPCS)
  about 210, 219
  and PhpStorm 220, 221
  URL, for downloading .tgz file 220
  URL, for sample ruleset file 223
  working 222, 223
PHPDoc 58
PHP Mess Detector (PHPMD)
  about 210, 211
  and PhpStorm 211-214
  rules 215, 216
  ruleset file, creating 218, 219
  URL 211
PHP method
  creating 45-48
PHP project
  creating, Composer used 36-41

PHP SSH2 extension 191
PhpStorm
  about 8, 211
  and PHPCS 220, 221
  and PHPMD 211-214
  code coverage 140-143
  connecting, to VCS repository 150, 151
  customization, performing with 26, 27
  Phing, connecting with 180-182
  plugin, configuring with 204, 205
PhpStorm application
  building, Phing used 186-188
PhpStorm project
  storing, in VCS repository 151-153
PHPUnit
  about 120
  application, testing with 124-126
  installing 120-122
  test case, creating 122
  test case, working 123, 124
PHPUnit class
  creating 122
plugin
  code hinting 205, 206
  configuring, with PhpStorm 204, 205
  engineering decisions, for creating 199
  refining 202-204
practical usage, Phing 190-193
previous edit location
  accessing 20
previous editor
  using 19
programming-related tasks 155, 156
project
  checking, out of VCS repository 166-168
  code, searching in 79-83
  empty project, creating 41
  existing project, renaming 41, 42
project file
  accessing 16, 17
project-settings section, PHP
  Debugger 63
  Directories 63
  Inspections 63
  Interpreter 63
  PHP Specific Settings 63

  Version Control 63
  Webserver 63
Project view 10
Property Prompt 193

R

RegEx 84
rules, PHPMD
  code size rules 215
  controversial rules 216
  cyclomatic complexity 215
  design rules 216
  excessive method length rule 216
  naming rules 217
  Npath complexity 215
  unused code rules 217
run configuration
  setting 88-92

S

section of code
  commenting out 58-62
setter method
  adding 49, 50
software engineering 210
source control 146
stepping through code process 134, 135
string
  wrapping 57, 58
Surround 53
svnadmin command 149
svnserve command 150
switches
  -a 89
  -B<begin_code> 89
  -c<path>|<file> 89
  -d foo[=bar] 89
  -e 89
  -E<end_code> 89
  -f<file> 89
  -F<file> 89
  -h 89
  -H 89
  -i 89

--ini 89
-l 89
-m 89
-n 89
--rc<name> 89
-r<code> 89
-R<code> 89
--re<name> 89
--rf<name> 89
--ri<name> 89
--rz<name> 89
-s 89
-S<addr>:<port> 89
-t<docroot> 89
-v 89
-w 89
-z<file> 89
args... 89

Symfony
  about 96
  controller, creating with 101-103
  directory structure 99, 100
  model, creating with 103-105
  URL, for downloading 97
  view, creating with 106, 107
  working with 97-99

T

task
  creating, for team 176-178
temporary breakpoint 130
Terminal view 9
test case 122
test case, PHPUnit
  creating 122
  working 123, 124
testing 120
testing system (PHPUnit) 140
test resource 31
TODO tag 64
TODO tasks
  creating 64, 65
TODO view 9
try-catch block 55
TWIG 106

U

unit testing 119
unwanted directories
  excluding, from index 30, 31

V

variable
  moving 75-77
  watching 138, 139
VCS 146
VCS repository
  code, synchronizing with 160-162
  code, updating from 157-160
  creating 148, 149
  examining 163-165
  files, committing to 154, 155
  PhpStorm, connecting to 150, 151
  PhpStorm project, storing in 151-153
  projects, checking out of 166-168
VCS server
  obtaining 146, 147
VCS tags
  creating 172-176
version control 146
version control system. *See* **VCS**
views
  about 8
  creating, with Symfony 106, 107
  creating, with Yii framework 110, 111
  creating, with Zend framework 114-116
  customizing 10, 11
  Database view 10
  displaying 8, 9
  Favorites view 10
  hiding 8, 9
  linking, to editors 20
  maximizing 17
  Project view 10
  Structure view 10
  Terminal view 9
  TODO view 9

W

watching 138
working set
  creating 62, 63

X

Xdebug 90, 127

Y

Yii framework
  controller, creating with 109
  model, creating with 107, 108
  view, creating with 110, 111

Z

zend-debugger 90
Zend framework
  controller, creating with 113, 114
  model, creating with 111-113
  view, creating with 114-116

About Packt Publishing

Packt, pronounced 'packed', published its first book, *Mastering phpMyAdmin for Effective MySQL Management*, in April 2004, and subsequently continued to specialize in publishing highly focused books on specific technologies and solutions.

Our books and publications share the experiences of your fellow IT professionals in adapting and customizing today's systems, applications, and frameworks. Our solution-based books give you the knowledge and power to customize the software and technologies you're using to get the job done. Packt books are more specific and less general than the IT books you have seen in the past. Our unique business model allows us to bring you more focused information, giving you more of what you need to know, and less of what you don't.

Packt is a modern yet unique publishing company that focuses on producing quality, cutting-edge books for communities of developers, administrators, and newbies alike. For more information, please visit our website at www.packtpub.com.

Writing for Packt

We welcome all inquiries from people who are interested in authoring. Book proposals should be sent to author@packtpub.com. If your book idea is still at an early stage and you would like to discuss it first before writing a formal book proposal, then please contact us; one of our commissioning editors will get in touch with you.

We're not just looking for published authors; if you have strong technical skills but no writing experience, our experienced editors can help you develop a writing career, or simply get some additional reward for your expertise.

Instant PhpStorm Starter

ISBN: 978-1-84969-394-3   Paperback: 86 pages

Learn professional PHP development with PhpStorm

1. Learn something new in an Instant! A short, fast, focused guide delivering immediate results.

2. Learn PhpStorm from scratch, from downloading to installation with no prior knowledge required.

3. Enter, modify, and inspect the source code with as much automation as possible.

4. Simple, full of easy-to-follow procedures and intuitive illustrations, this book will set you speedily on the right track.

Mastering TypoScript
TYPO3 Website, Template, and Extension Development

ISBN: 978-1-90481-197-8   Paperback: 400 pages

A complete guide to understanding and using TypoScript, TYPO3's powerful configuration language

1. Powerful control and customization using TypoScript.

2. Covers templates, extensions, admin, interface, menus, and database control.

3. You don't need to be an experienced PHP developer to use the power of TypoScript.

Please check **www.PacktPub.com** for information on our titles

www.ingramcontent.com/pod-product-compliance
Lightning Source LLC
Chambersburg PA
CBHW060540060326
40690CB00017B/3550